THE POETRY OF EMILY DICKINSON

OXFORD STUDIES IN PHILOSOPHY AND LITERATURE

Richard Eldridge, Philosophy, Swarthmore College

PUBLISHED IN THE SERIES

THE POETRY OF EMILY DICKINSON

Philosophical Perspectives

Edited by Elisabeth Camp

OXFORD
UNIVERSITY PRESS

OXFORD
UNIVERSITY PRESS

Oxford University Press is a department of the University of Oxford. It furthers
the University's objective of excellence in research, scholarship, and education
by publishing worldwide. Oxford is a registered trade mark of Oxford University
Press in the UK and certain other countries.

Published in the United States of America by Oxford University Press
198 Madison Avenue, New York, NY 10016, United States of America.

Library of Congress Cataloging-in-Publication Data
Names: Camp, Elisabeth, editor.
Title: The poetry of Emily Dickinson : philosophical perspectives /
Edited by Elisabeth Camp.
Description: New York, NY : Oxford University Press, [2021] |
Series: Oxford studies in philosophy and literature |
Includes bibliographical references and index.
Identifiers: LCCN 2020027496 (print) | LCCN 2020027497 (ebook) |
ISBN 9780190651190 (hardback) | ISBN 9780190651206 (paperback) |
ISBN 9780190651220 (epub)
Subjects: LCSH: Dickinson, Emily, 1830–1886—Criticism and interpretation. |
Dickinson, Emily, 1830–1886—Philosophy. | Philosophy in literature.
Classification: LCC PS1541.Z5 .P55 2020 (print) |
LCC PS1541.Z5 (ebook) | DDC 811/.4—dc23
LC record available at https://lccn.loc.gov/2020027496
LC ebook record available at https://lccn.loc.gov/2020027497

DOI: 10.1093/oso/9780190651190.001.0001

1 3 5 7 9 8 6 4 2

Paperback printed by Marquis, Canada
Hardback printed by Bridgeport National Bindery, Inc., United States of America

CONTENTS

SERIES EDITOR'S FOREWORD

At least since Plato had Socrates criticize the poets and attempt to displace Homer as the authoritative articulator and transmitter of human experience and values, philosophy and literature have developed as partly competing, partly complementary enterprises. Both literary writers and philosophers have frequently studied and commented on each other's texts and ideas, sometimes with approval, sometimes with disapproval, in their efforts to become clearer about human life and about valuable commitments—moral, artistic, political, epistemic, metaphysical, and religious, as may be. Plato's texts themselves register the complexity and importance of these interactions in being dialogues in which both deductive argumentation and dramatic narration do central work in furthering a complex body of views.

While these relations have been widely recognized, they have also frequently been ignored or misunderstood, as academic disciplines have gone their separate ways within their modern institutional settings. Philosophy has often turned to science or mathematics as providing models of knowledge; in doing so it has often explicitly set itself against cultural entanglements and literary devices, rejecting, at least officially, the importance of plot, figuration, and imagery in favor of supposedly plain speech about the truth. Literary study has moved variously through formalism, structuralism, post-structuralism, and cultural studies, among other movements, as modes of approach to a literary text. In doing so it has understood literary texts as sample instances of images, structures, personal styles, or failures of consciousness, or it has seen the literary text as a largely fungible product, fundamentally shaped by wider pressures and patterns of consumption and expectation that affect and figure in non-literary textual production as well. It has thus set itself against the idea that major literary texts productively and originally address philosophical problems of value and commitment precisely through their form, diction, imagery, and development, even while these works also resist claiming conclusively to solve the problems that occupy them.

These distinct academic traditions have yielded important perspectives and insights. But in the end none of them has been kind to the idea of major literary works as achievements in thinking about values and human life, often in distinctive, open, self-revising, self-critical ways. At the same time readers outside institutional settings, and often enough philosophers and literary scholars too, have turned to major literary texts precisely in order to engage with their productive, materially and medially specific patterns and processes of thinking. These turns to literature have, however, not so far been systematically encouraged within disciplines, and they have generally occurred independently of each other.

The aim of this series is to make manifest the multiple, complex engagements with philosophical ideas and problems that lie at the hearts of major literary texts. In doing so, its volumes aim not only to help philosophers and literary scholars of various kinds to find rich affinities and provocations to further thought and work, they also aim to bridge various gaps between academic disciplines and between those disciplines and the experiences of extra-institutional readers.

Each volume focuses on a single, undisputedly major literary text. Both philosophers with training and experience in literary study and literary scholars with training and experience in philosophy are invited to engage with themes, details, images, and incidents in the focal text, through which philosophical problems are held in view, worried at, and reformulated. Decidedly not a project simply to formulate A's philosophy of X as a finished product, merely illustrated in the text, and decidedly not a project to explain the literary work entirely by reference to external social configurations and forces, the effort is instead to track the work of open thinking in literary forms, as they lie both neighbor to and aslant from philosophy. As Walter Benjamin once wrote, "new centers of reflection are continually forming," as problems of commitment and value of all kinds take on new shapes for human agents in relation to changing historical circumstances, where reflective address remains possible. By considering how such centers of reflection are formed and expressed in and through literary works, as they engage with philosophical problems of agency, knowledge, commitment, and value, these volumes undertake to present both literature and philosophy as, at times, productive forms of reflective, medial work in relation both to each other and to social circumstances and to show how this work is specifically undertaken and developed in distinctive and original ways in exemplary works of literary art.

Richard Eldridge
Swarthmore College

CONTRIBUTORS

Antony Aumann is Associate Professor of Philosophy at Northern Michigan University. He has previously held positions at The Ohio State University, St. Olaf College, and Fordham University in the Bronx. Aumann's research engages both the continental and analytic traditions of philosophy, and he specializes in issues related to aesthetics, existentialism, and religion. His work has appeared in journals and collections such as *The Kierkegaardian Mind, Journal of Aesthetics and Art Criticism,* and *Continental Philosophy Review.* His 2019 monograph with Rowman & Littlefield is entitled *Art and Selfhood: A Kierkegaardian Account.* Aumann is also the co-editor of New Kierkegaard Research, a series of monographs and edited collections published by Lexington Books.

Rick Anthony Furtak is Associate Professor of Philosophy at Colorado College. The main areas of his research are the philosophy of emotions, existential thought (in particular, Kierkegaard and his legacy), and the contested relationship between philosophy and literature. His books include *Rilke's "Sonnets to Orpheus": A New English Version, with a Philosophical Introduction* (2007), *Thoreau's*

Importance for Philosophy (2012), and most recently *Knowing Emotions: Truthfulness and Recognition in Affective Experience* (2018). He is currently writing about love and subjectivity in the work of Proust.

David Hills is Associate Professor of Philosophy (Teaching) at Stanford University, having previously taught at Harvard University; University of California, Los Angeles; University of Pennsylvania; University of Michigan, Ann Arbor; and University of California, Berkeley. He has written and spoken widely on aesthetics, philosophy of mind, philosophy of language, and the history of modern philosophy, especially Kant and Wittgenstein. He prepared a bibliography on metaphor for Oxford Bibliographies in 2018 and is at work on two books: one on metaphor and the other on Kant's *Critique of the Power of Judgment.*

Oren Izenberg is Associate Professor in the Department of English at University of California, Irvine. His research focuses on the long history of poetry and poetics, and on intersections between literary and philosophical explorations of personhood, mind, and action. He is the author of *Being Numerous: Poetry and the Ground of Social Life* (2011), and a member of the editorial board of *nonsite.*

Eileen John is Reader in Philosophy at the University of Warwick. Her research is in aesthetics and philosophy of literature, and she has broad interests in art and values. She has directed Warwick's Centre for Research in Philosophy, Literature and the Arts, and co-edited the Blackwell anthology "The Philosophy of Literature: Contemporary and Classic Readings."

Magdalena Ostas has served on the faculty in the English Department at Rhode Island College, Boston University, and Florida Atlantic University. She works and teaches at the crossroads of nineteenth-century literature and literature, philosophy, and the arts, and has written on a range of figures at this intersection, including Kant, Wordsworth, Keats, Jane Austen, Nietzsche, Wittgenstein, Stanley Cavell, Jeff Wall, and Michael Fried. Her essays have appeared in *International Studies in Philosophy*, *symploke*, *Studies in Romanticism*, and *nonsite* and in the collections *Michael Fried and Philosophy* and *MLA Approaches to Teaching Jane Austen's* Persuasion. She is at work on a study about art, expression, and interior life in poetry, philosophy, and the novel around 1800.

Introduction

Emily Dickinson's Epistemic Ambitions for Poetry

ELISABETH CAMP

All of the contributors to this volume argue that poetry is capable of a kind of epistemic achievement, and that Emily Dickinson in particular is an epistemically ambitious poet. On the view that emerges, poetry is a means for getting a better grip on how the world is and one's place within it; and Dickinson uses poetry both to understand the world and to advocate for poetry as a tool of understanding. Many of the contributors also argue that Dickinson offers a distinctive construal of what knowledge is: as an ongoing, inevitably unfinished process rather than a fixed state. The unfinished nature of knowledge, on this view, arises in part because the world transcends complete grasp by any finite agent, and in part because as long as the knowing agent is alive, she is never a complete, static entity. But it arises especially because the species of robust connection to reality required for knowledge is something that must be continually earned, through daily cognitive, emotional, and practical labor.

Some aspects of the resulting portrait fit smoothly with the stereotype of Dickinson as a reclusive poet. She has an acute sense of a

The Poetry of Emily Dickinson. Elisabeth Camp, Oxford University Press (2021). © Oxford University Press.
DOI: 10.1093/oso/9780190651190.003.0001

gulf between herself and the rest of the world. She engages in close observation of nature and of her own mental states. She is especially concerned with "small moments" and creatures in nature—birds, snakes, frost—and with the "what it's like" of pain and death. But the Dickinson we encounter here is also decidedly more determined, argumentative, and hopeful than that stereotype allows. She strides "Vast Prairies of Air" in search of a "Missing All." She instructs her audience on aspects of reality they have ignored. Although the promised "All" is elusive, she at least sometimes finds the right words in the right form to situate herself at home in the world. And when understanding does fail her, so that her cognitive and emotional "strings are snapt," she doesn't give up, but gets back up and sets herself to work.

This portrait of Dickinson as a striving, inquisitive poet stands in stark contrast to the more pessimistic, even nihilistic construal of Dickinson articulated by many recent interpreters. Ted Hughes, for instance, characterizes her as in the grip of "almost a final revelation of horrible Nothingness," such that

> Remaining true to this, she could make up her mind about nothing. . . . Registering everywhere and in everything the icy chill of its nearness, she did not know what to think . . . all other concerns floated free of finality, became merely relative, susceptible to her artistic play.[1]

Moreover, this portrait of Dickinson as an epistemically ambitious poet also provides us with substantive lessons for philosophy itself, by offering alternative characterizations of what knowledge is, and of the methodologies through which it can be achieved.

1. Hughes, "Introduction to *A Choice of Emily Dickinson's Verse*," 358–359; cited in John, ch. 6 of this volume.

The first essay in the volume, by *Rick Anthony Furtak*, focuses on Dickinson's attitudes toward knowledge of the external world, especially God and nature. The poet's initial findings are skeptical: when she sets out to find a person-like God who inspects our actions from his residence in Heaven, and who we will eventually encounter face-to-face after death, Dickinson encounters no "sign" from which she can "infer his Residence," only "Vast Prairies of Air / Unbroken by a Settler." However, when she pauses in this "Infinitude," she finds that the "Silence" "condescends" to "stop for her," and she is awed to encounter a Creation that transcends what she sought. Similarly, when Dickinson observes practices of institutionalized prayer in church, she finds only empty religious vestments and incantations. But when she "keeps the Sabbath" by "staying at Home" in her garden, guided by the local songbirds, then she is on her way toward Heaven "all along."

Furtak thus locates Dickinson as belonging to Emerson and Thoreau's Transcendentalist tradition of "natural supernaturalism," on which being perceptually and emotionally attuned to nature is the only authentic form of worship. Dickinson does at least sometimes feel she knows the reality of divinity, and more generally of a meaningful external world, in a way that is "immediately present as a fact of experience, available to those who have ears to hear and eyes to see," as Furtak says. At the same time, it is not easy, nor always possible, to maintain this confidence, for at least two reasons.

First, Dickinson's epistemic confidence is grounded in a suite of feelings—of awe and wonder, and of being "at home"—which one must experience firsthand. One can "keep the Sabbath" by implementing practices of mindful attention that make these feelings more likely. But how one feels is not ultimately under one's control; and the poet does frequently feel estranged from her social and natural environments: a "Stranger[] in a foreign World."

3

Second, even when these feelings are present, Dickinson worries that they are mere projections onto an empty void, and hence self-gratifying delusions rather than epistemic achievements. Thus, in

> To hear an Oriole sing
> May be a common thing -
> Or only a divine.

she suggests that it is possible that the "Tune" or "Rune" of an Oriole's song—its being a melody, being beautiful, and/or having its being a sign of the divine—is "only" a matter of interpretation, rather than of "common" fact: something that depends on how the "Fashion of the Ear" "attires" bare sound waves, rather than a feature inherent in reality, ready to be discovered.

Interpreters like Farhang Erfani[2] take such passages to establish that Dickinson embraces the skeptical conclusion that there is a fundamental gap between us and the world, and that meaning and divinity are merely human projections. Furtak agrees that the skeptic's hypothesis, combined with the poet's own firsthand experiences of meaning as fluctuating in accordance with her "Mood," invalidates a naïve view that the "song" is real in an absolute, objective sense; but he argues that they leave open the possibility that the song is a joint creation of bird and listener. On this neo-Kantian reading, a mind that is properly attuned to nature is genuinely responding to something external to itself which it cloaks in distinctively human form, so that "in the meeting of mind and world, both the subject and the object make essential contributions."

A key reason for taking Dickinson to reject the skeptical conclusion is that she consistently takes Nature to transcend our powers

---

2. See, e.g., Erfani, "Dickinson and Sartre on Facing the Brutality of Brute Existence," cited in Furtak, ch. 1 of this volume.

of perception and understanding. Like the philosophers, Dickinson craves knowledge; and she takes their methodology of analysis and inference very seriously. But to endorse the skeptical conclusion, one would need first, to accept the assumption that our cognitive capacities are indeed adequate to analyze the evidence we acquire through perception, and second, to infer from this that an oriole's chirp is nothing more than bare sounds mis-dressed by us with merely mental "attire." And for Dickinson, such an assumption of epistemic adequacy is undermined: first, by her frequent negative experiences of limitation in the course of "this timid life of Evidence"; and second, by her positive albeit intermittent experiences of divine transcendence:

> This World is not Conclusion
> A Species stands beyond -
> Invisible, as Music -
> But positive, as Sound -

For Furtak's Dickinson, then, we are essentially finite beings stuck in a perpetual state of epistemic in-between-ness. This is not just agnosticism, understood as the refusal to endorse either a positive or negative conclusion about the reality of divinity (or of melody, or of sound). Rather, it is an active condition of "Wonder," of "not precisely Knowing / And not precisely Knowing not": a search for understanding that can only ever be partially accomplished. Further, in contrast to philosophers, who fetishize analysis and inference and take themselves to know only what they can conclude via those means, Dickinson takes herself to have other epistemic tools at her disposal. We've already seen that she appeals to first-person experiences of awe and comfort. But as Furtak notes, and as Hills will argue at greater length, she also takes it that in those cases where "Philosophy - don't know," some measure of "Sagacity" can still be achieved by going "through a Riddle," in the distinctive manner afforded by poetry.

In considering why the ultimate reality of nature and God should transcend our finite epistemic capacities, it is natural to focus on the fact that they are outside of, and in this sense "other" to, us. But as *Magdalena Ostas* argues, Dickinson often finds her own self to be at least as mysterious as the external world: "Ourself behind ourself, concealed - Should startle most," as she says. Indeed, the "self" she discerns is sometimes almost comically "haunted": her mind and brain are "cleaved," full of hidden "corridors," and divided across time in a way that leaves her brain "giggling" at the "odd" mismatch between "That person that I was - And this One." Such internal "otherness" makes the sort of introspection required for self-knowledge into a monumentally challenging task. In particular, much as with Dickinson's confrontation with nature's "Vast Prairies of Air," so too does examining her own self require not just precise attentiveness, but also emotional courage in the face of alienation:

I do not know the man so bold
He dare in lonely Place
That awful stranger - Consciousness
Deliberately face -

Passages like this might seem to supply clear grounds for attributing a nihilistic vision to Dickinson. Perhaps, as Geoffrey Hartmann claims, Dickinson's "spectatorial" gaze is a coping mechanism which allows her to "elide the agony of self-consciousness."[3] Or perhaps she has mustered the courage to introspect, and has discovered that there lurks only an empty void, rendering her own life irrevocably "other." However, much as Furtak argues that Dickinson entertains but

---

3. Hartmann, "Language from the Point of View of Literature," 350, cited in Ostas, ch. 3 of this volume.

ultimately rejects external-world skepticism in favor of a neo-Kantian constructivism about nature, so Ostas argues that Dickinson rejects epistemic and metaphysical pessimisms about the mental in favor of an innovative form of self-constructivism.

To see why, it helps to bracket questions of self-knowledge for a moment, to first consider what self-expression means for Dickinson. Given Dickinson's frequent interest in close observation of inner states, there is a persistent tendency to read her as a broadly "confessional" poet: an intrepid phenomenological ornithologist documenting shy species of *qualia* in order to place them on display for the rest of the world. Along similar lines, it is tempting to read Dickinson's many poems about death, such as "I heard a Fly buzz - when I died ," as attempts to accurately simulate qualitative states that are real but otherwise cognitively inaccessible.

As we will see in discussing Izenberg's contribution, it is plausible that Dickinson is at least sometimes engaged in such projects of documentation and simulation. But Ostas argues that Dickinson's poems of self-expression are more actively creative than the confessional model allows. More specifically, she argues that Dickinson's frequent trope of "self-splitting" does not function (just) to diagnose an antecedently existing state of alienation between multiple personalities, but instead serves as an imaginative technique for "serious, forceful investigation," in which the poet "dares" to stage various possibilities, in order to probe how they strike her.

More specifically, Ostas argues that in writing her poems Dickinson assigns herself the role of curious reader as much as that of documentary reporter. Poetry gives her "the Art to stun myself / With Bolts - of Melody!": that is, by "hear[ing] the words as they make an entry into the world, suddenly concrete, as though they had not issued from her own pen and voice," Dickinson gains a new, alternative perspective on the thoughts and attitudes they express. Just as Dickinson inspects her bodily features, like her hair and dimples, to see whether they "twinkle back / Conviction . . . of me - ," so too she "turns [her] Being round and round" verbally in her poetry:

> I felt my life with both my hands
> To see if it was there -
> I held my spirit to the Glass,
> To prove it possibler -

Confronting herself with the "sounds" she generates in her writing thus provides the poet with a mechanism for assessing whether she can accept the contents they express as her "own."

Instead of deploying "a logic of pressing thoughts or feelings outward from inside," then, Ostas takes Dickinson to exemplify a model of self-expression as self-construction—a model that has also been articulated by philosophers like Stanley Cavell, Charles Taylor, and Richard Eldridge. On this view, the task of self-expression is as much epistemic as it is communicative. But beyond this, self-expression also becomes a constitutive project of constructing a self, for at least two reasons. First, at a local level, verbal articulation helps to make the particular feelings and thoughts expressed into what they are, by assigning them a form and a location in relation to a network of other possible and actual feelings and thoughts. Indeed, Ostas argues that insofar as their verbal articulation essentially contributes to constituting those thoughts and feelings, the self they express is distributed externally, on the page. Second and more globally, the poet's response to the thoughts and feelings she "stages" at least partially constitutes them as hers: she embraces some as belonging to her, at least for this moment, while marginalizing others as odd, past, merely simulated, or otherwise "other."

This constructivist model of self-expression and selfhood in turn produces a model of self-knowledge that neatly echoes the constructivist account of nature articulated by Furtak. In both the outer and inner realms, our contributors attribute to Dickinson a view of knowledge as a relationship, one that must be continually achieved by a highly complex but limited self grappling to make contact with a transcendently complex reality. And in both cases, the way in which the self receives and interprets that reality partially, but only partially, constitutes it as reality. Further, both Furtak and Ostas argue that in this quest, inner sensations and emotional responses function not just as objects of knowledge, but also as epistemic tools. The poet begins with a felt yearning to understand: an often "irritable" curiosity "That nibbles at the soul." Like the philosopher, she observes, infers, and hypothesizes from the evidence she accumulates. But this never suffices: knowledge, when it comes, involves an immediate feeling of kinship, one which can be cultivated but not summoned and that is often elusive.

Where Furtak and Ostas argue that Dickinson embraces the possibility of partial knowledge in the face of skeptical threats, *Oren Izenberg* tackles the more basic question of whether poetry in general, and Dickinson in particular, are even in the business of attempting to achieve knowledge. Echoing Francis Bacon, who claimed that poetry "is rather a pleasure or play of imagination, than a work or duty thereof,"[4] many theorists of disparate stripes today hold that poetry lacks any (warranted) epistemic ambition. Instead, they take it either to be just another entry in the field of "cultural production," interesting for what it reveals about its sociopolitical environment; or else to function as an antidote to reality, "resisting by its form alone the course of the world, which permanently puts a pistol to men's heads," as Adorno says.[5]

Against this, Izenberg argues that an interest in poetry is justified by a manifest, albeit typically implicit, commitment by poets

4. Bacon, *Advancement of Learning*, 82, cited in Izenberg, ch. 3 of this volume.
5. Adorno, "Commitment," 78, cited in Izenberg, ch. 3 of this volume.

themselves to "epistemic payoff." This, he claims, is what poets usually present themselves as doing, and what we as readers usually take them to be doing. Redeeming this commitment requires fending off a classic pair of threats. On the one hand, if a poem merely records what one person once happened to think or feel on one occasion, then it offers nothing more than an entry in a cabinet of curiosities, unverifiable by and uninteresting for others. But on the other hand, if the poem achieves general applicability by being stripped of its specificities, then the content that remains is typically either a banal triviality, a substantive fact known only on the basis of some other source of authority, or a patent falsehood.

One option for avoiding this dichotomy is to claim that poems propose possibilities, in the form of thought experiments. On its own, this might not seem like a marked improvement over the cabinet of curiosities. Given the vast expanse of modal space, merely knowing that one's conception is metaphysically possible is disappointingly meager reward: we want to know, and poets appear to take themselves to offer, some insight into how this world actually is.

Izenberg claims that the payoff is more substantive, and that the very features of lyric poetry that make it seem remote from genuine knowledge are in fact sources of epistemic value. His argument proceeds by way of an analogy, or a "pleasing, if slant rhyme," between lyric poems and David Chalmers's "Cosmoscope." Chalmers aims to resuscitate the Leibnitzian/Laplacean dream that an ideal reasoner could know everything about the world by knowing a highly restricted, privileged subclass of truths about it. To motivate the plausibility of such an accomplishment, and to get a grip on what it would involve, Chalmers suggests that we imagine possessing a virtual reality device into which all the facts of the world have been entered, and which has the power to calculate all entailments of those facts. Such a device wouldn't do anything that a non-ideal reasoner couldn't accomplish in principle; it "simply offloads" some of the burden of storage and calculation "from ourselves onto the world." But armed with such a device, "one could come to know anything that could be known."[6]

Similarly, Izenberg suggests, many lyric poems should be treated as "investigatory devices" that deploy poetic rhetorical performances to provide evidence about a restricted base of facts, from which the poet and readers can draw inferences. More specifically, he argues that Dickinson makes contributions to each of the four classes of facts that Chalmers identifies as inputs to the Cosmoscope. These are first, the class of micro- and macrophysical *physical* truths and their governing laws; second, the class of *phenomenological* or experiential truths: what it's like to be in various psychological states, plus the psychophysical laws connecting them to matter; third, a class of *indexical* truths, specifying where and when one actually is; and finally, a "that's all" clause, affirming that P, Q, and I exhaust the *totality* of truths.

First, in the domain of physical facts, Izenberg argues that Dickinson deploys the laser-like focus of poetry to home in on specific aspects of nature. One such technique presents "ribbons" of time, much as a time-lapse camera records an unfolding empirical "Experiment":

> At half-past Three
> a single Bird
> Unto a silent Sky
> Propounded but a single
> term
> Of cautious melody -

By focusing attention on a sequence of temporal moments, the poet is able to observe the details of those moments as simultaneously separate and connected, in a way that "allows space for the drawing

6. Chalmers, *Constructing the World*, 117, cited in Izenberg, ch. 3 of this volume.

of inferences from data." Similarly, in poems like "Ashes denote that Fire / was" Dickinson infers from what she sees at one moment to something unobserved in the past—while also, as we've seen, noting the limits of what can be grasped through analysis and inference.

Within the second class, of phenomenological truths, we have already seen that Dickinson is often concerned to describe actual and possible phenomenological states that confound comprehension, especially pain and madness, with a precise particularity absent from ordinary language. Much like Ostas, Izenberg argues that Dickinson frequently strives to draw experiences that are unnameable in virtue of being noncognitive and phenomenal —for instance, Pain, which "has an Element of Blank"—into the realm of knowledge by imposing partial, provisional conceptualizations on them. Crucially, Izenberg argues, the poet doesn't merely describe, but actually instances those experiences within the poem. Thus, in "I felt a Funeral, in my Brain," we don't just learn that Dickinson felt an experience which was like hearing "Mourners" treading with "Boots of Lead"; we feel the pounding, numbing repetition in the poem's own sounds. By conveying experience via exemplification, poetry escapes the worrisome limitations of self-report. And by inducing analogous imaginative states in its readers, such poems offer an opportunity for knowledge of experiences as "idiosyncratic but not private": as indexed to a highly specific, but not essentially individual, context.

Third, also in the indexical class, Izenberg argues that first-person lyric poetry is invested in anchoring the speaker to specific locations in space and time by pointing to their context of utterance, in a way that enables the reader to instantiate for themselves contexts that are similar in relevant respects to the speaker's, as for example in

This is a Blossom of
the Brain -
A small - italic Seed.

As we saw, Ostas also drew attention to the importance of context in Dickinson's poems, and to the way that indexicality can bridge the gap between speaker and audience. However, where Ostas focuses on Dickinson's own role as reader, testing whether she can encompass the described experiences at the moment of reception, Izenberg argues that Dickinson's indexical elements point toward a more broadly available "fictive present": a possible here-and-now that other readers can implement for themselves, through actual re-enactment or imaginative projection.

Finally—in marked contrast to Furtak and Ostas—Izenberg claims that what he calls "figures of totality" are "endemic" to lyric poetry in general and to Dickinson's poems in particular. Here he cites Dickinson's common invocations of noon as "an hour of undivided illumination that leaves nothing in shadow," and her frequent skepticism of anything like Heaven as an undisclosed domain inaccessible to thought, as in:

> I have no
> Life but this -
> To lead it
> here -
> Nor any Death -
> but lest
> Dispelled from
> there -

If we grant that Dickinson does make entries into each of Chalmers's four categories, what does the "slant rhyme" with the Cosmoscope show? Dickinson and other lyric poets obviously shouldn't, and don't, claim to have amassed the kind of complete privileged data set that would fuel a Leibnitzian/Laplacean reasoning engine. Rather, Izenberg takes the analogy with the Cosmoscope to show that lyric poets like Dickinson are making potentially valuable contributions to the project of achieving knowledge. First, they are using their powers of observation, description, and imagination to furnish actual reasoners—at least themselves, and often their (other) readers—with the same basic types of data that ordinary epistemic agents typically invoke. Second, they are deploying their cognitive powers of reason and imagination to amplify that base into a more compendious set. And third, they are doing so in the service of a sincere investigation into reality.

Indeed, the fact that lyric poetry typically presents its contents in what Chalmers calls an "empirical" rather than "conditional" mode—as claims about actuality rather than speculations about what would follow if certain states were to be actual—suggests that poetry may provide a more promising basis for establishing aesthetic "cognitivism" than fiction, which has been the more common target of philosophers' interrogations of learning from literature. For her own personal Cosmoscopic purposes, the poet needs no independent verification of the phenomena she encounters. She knows directly that she has experienced them; her challenge is to articulate them in a form that renders them comprehensible to her, and to test whether she can affirm them as reflective of a wider, persisting reality. Thus, for a poet like Dickinson, the possibility that her experiences are highly particular, even idiosyncratic may not be troubling: like Descartes in the *Meditations*, her epistemic ambitions may be directed simply at comprehending the world around and within her, for her own sake. For other poets—Walt Whitman, say—the overt need for affirmation in a common experience with other people is more central. In either case, regardless of the poet's intentions and desires, a reader may use a poem's data and its associative connections as scaffolding for their own epistemic projects, by directing their attention toward the same species of phenomena the poet has noticed, by marshaling their conceptual and imaginative resources in the same types of structures, and by tracing out the same types of inferential patterns.

WHY POETRY?

So far, our contributors have focused on establishing that poets like Dickinson are seeking knowledge in some recognizable sense of the term. But if that is their aim, why should we think that they are doing a good job: that their ambitions are sufficiently well placed that we as readers, and perhaps specifically as philosophers, should take them seriously in those terms? More specifically, Furtak, Ostas, and Izenberg all argue that Dickinson and other poets are presenting contents or claims about philosophically interesting topics like the ontological status of God, or the self, or the expressibility of phenomenal states. But granting them this status threatens to undermine their value as poets. Why are they not then just doing mediocre philosophy, cloaked in cumbersome fancy attire?

Here, it is useful to distinguish two subsidiary questions. First, if poets like Dickinson are attempting to supply the same basic types of claims as other folks inquiring after truth, why should they articulate those contents in such a strange way? Call this the question of *poetic form and content*. Second, how does the form and status of lyric poetry affect the epistemic status of those claims? In Izenberg's Chalmersian terms, supposing that poets do supply the Cosmoscope with contents as input, why think that poetry makes any distinctive contribution over and above the usual labor of churning out truths through standard inference rules? Call this the question of *poetic form and justification*.

Poetic Form and Content

While some poets, such as Alexander Pope, may be justly accused of making versified philosophy, Dickinson insists that her truth must be told "slant": that to write in more standard prose would be a form of "shutting her up," of locking her in a cognitive "closet." Why is this? What difference does how she writes make to what she does?

We have already encountered one reason why Dickinson can't put her point "straight": many of the states she is interested in defy adequate categorization with ordinary concepts. As Izenberg argues, many phenomenological states, especially pain, have an "Element of Blank" which the poet attempts to fill in, or at least delineate, using non-literal tropes like metaphor. Further, as Ostas argues, in at least some of these cases the process of articulation involves not just matching stable inner states to either conventional or occasion-specific word meanings, but partially constituting those mental states themselves.

However, the ineffability of phenomenal states covers only a small portion of Dickinson's expressive choices. What other motivations are there for poetic form, and what implications might this have for how we might integrate Dickinson's insights into our own philosophizing? *Antony Aumann* argues that in an important sense, Dickinson "had to write how she did"; but that this is compatible with what she says being paraphrased in ordinary terms. Building on Martha Nussbaum's insight that "form is not always neutral,"[7] he argues that a speaker's use of a certain form can contribute to the content they express, by implying acceptance of a perspective which in turn entails certain propositional contents. Prosaically, this is illustrated by the way a speaker's choice of gender-neutral or

7. Nussbaum, "Form and Content, Philosophy and Literature," in *Love's Knowledge*, 15; cited in Aumann, ch. 4 of this volume.

-specific pronouns reveals their attitudes toward certain assumptions about gender equality. Poetically, Aumann argues, it is manifested by Dickinson's use of "hymn scheme": an A-B-A-B rhyming pattern plus a 4-3-4-3 or "common" meter with iambic stresses. Because hymn scheme was strongly associated with Puritanism in 19th-century New England, and because Dickinson was herself deeply enmeshed in Puritan ideas and images, it is expressively appropriate for her to employ this form. But at the same time, insofar as a "straight" deployment would imply straightforward endorsement of Puritan doctrine, this would be inappropriate given Dickinson's contentious relationship to established religion. Thus, her rhythmic and aural distortions of hymn scheme appropriately reflect her substantive attitude of challenging engagement with Puritanism.

Aumann argues that the operative notions of "appropriateness" and "inappropriateness" here are stronger than the sort of aesthetic harmony exemplified by the resemblances between, for instance, the repeated "s" sounds in "His notice sudden is" and the hissing of the snake being described, or between the slowing metrical pace induced by the increasing flurry of hyphens in "This is the Hour of Lead" and the described experience of freezing to death. It's not just that the form "fits" or fails to fit the expressed content. Rather, he argues, the choice to use a certain form can generate genuine propositional inconsistency via a "performative contradiction," much as using gender-specific language to articulate a progressive gender policy would.

What implications does this connection between form and content have for the feasibility of paraphrasing poetic contents? Aumann argues that while a candidate paraphrase may indeed fail to capture a poem's total intended effect, a paraphrase, in the "modest" sense of an approximate statement of a poem's main contents, is often both possible and legitimate. The formal expressive constraints under which poets operate are generated by the fact that they are engaged in a speech act of assertion, or something akin to it: "presenting their own views, perspectives, and attitudes about some subject matter." By contrast, because the act of reporting others' speech does not involve a commitment to the truth of the reported contents, it does not generate the same performative contradiction.

Aumann's diagnosis presupposes again that poets are in the epistemic business, and specifically that they are engaged in something like a conversation with their readers: proffering ideas that they take to be "right or true," and representing themselves as "standing behind or endorsing" them. Much like Izenberg, Aumann argues that abandoning this presupposition entails an implausibly widespread error theory about the interpretive practices of both scholarly and lay readers. But even if we grant that poets are epistemically ambitious, we might still want to deny that they are engaged specifically in assertion. In particular, Dickinson often appears to be raising questions without settling them, as Furtak claims; or staging possibilities to test whether she can affirm them, as Ostas argues. Alternatively, she may not be speaking in her own voice, but in that of "a supposed person," as she herself puts it. Aumann argues that none of these possibilities threatens the basic conversational model, or its consequence that poets operate under formal constraints that their interpreters don't. First, while some of Dickinson's poems are presented in a hypothetical or exploratory tone, others are more committal. Second and more importantly, even if Dickinson herself doesn't definitively endorse the contents she expresses, those constraints on performative consistency still apply to the speaking persona. (We might add that some models of communication and assertion-like acts, such as Stalnaker's, are designed to accommodate both exploratory and personified speech; and that expressive constraints are conditionally inherited by such speech.)

While the objection to assertoric force doesn't undermine the claim that poets often proffer contents in a way that commits them to performative consistency and epistemic assessment, it does bring out the importance of identifying the appropriate unit of assessment. At a superficial level, we should be careful about citing isolated passages as capturing "what Dickinson thinks"; rather—as with exegesis more generally—we need to analyze how those utterances function within their immediate contexts, and whether they reflect a broader position that the speaking persona expresses on other occasions. At a deeper level, if we accept Ostas's argument that expression for Dickinson is less a matter of "confessing," in the sense of offering an outward sign of an antecedently fixed inner state, and more a matter of grappling with a continual series of mental phenomena as candidates for affirmation, then we also need to question the simple conception of selves as stable entities who "stand behind" their assertions. While some might take this as the opening wedge for neo-Wittgensteinian skepticism about meaning and knowledge, we might also take it, as our contributors do, as the impetus to develop a more realistic and flexible model of knowledge and conversation generally.

Poetic Form and Justification

So far, we have canvassed two primary content-based reasons why poets in general and Dickinson in particular need to express themselves as they do: the inadequacy of any ordinary conventional substitute, especially for representing phenomenal states; and the requirement that one's mode of expression be minimally consistent with, and hopefully positively fitting for, the contents expressed.

In his contribution, *David Hills* focuses on a set of reasons for employing certain forms of expression which is related to the process of coming to understand a content. Even when the content in question can be coherently expressed in ordinary terms, he argues, engaging with the "Riddle" of poetry can afford a species of "Sagacity" not provided by direct articulation.

One of Dickinson's characteristic modes is to describe an object, like a hummingbird or frost, using a trope like metonymy and personification, in ways that seduce her reader into achieving a more "distinct sight" of that object, by piquing their curiosity about what it is that she might be talking about. In this way, expressive occlusion produces a kind of cognitive clarity:

The thought beneath so slight a film -
Is more distinctly seen -
As laces just reveal the surge -
Or Mists - the Apennine

In some of these "riddle" poems, the "mists" of allusion and unexpected detail help to bring a familiar object into focus, by highlighting its contours within our own established thinking; they clarify and reconfigure what we already know, rather than teaching us something new. In others, especially those employing extended metaphors, the riddle's target is less familiar, or less cognitively tractable. The riddle is then correspondingly less straightforward: it contains layers of observation and multiple, sometimes conflicting threads of interpretation. Hills argues that tracing out each of these threads forces the reader to spend extended time with the subject, by approaching it from multiple angles and assembling multiple distinct impressions into a whole that ultimately embodies a kind of stable cognitive coherence, albeit one that may not be straightforwardly logically consistent.

This latter approach is especially appropriate when the riddle's subject is something as amorphous and terrifying as death, as in a poem like

A Clock stopped -
Not the Mantel's -

In such cases, each successive layer of meaning informs and rewards the reader by staging a different "performance" of the metaphor; but it also entices and prepares the reader to move on to less familiar, obvious, and stable aspects, in what Hills calls "a process of demythologizing our initial understanding of its primary subject." The result is "metaphors that owe their lasting effectiveness as metaphors to their temporary effectiveness as euphemisms." The poem's indirectness underwrites an epistemic gain even in cases where the "whole truth" could in principle be articulated directly, because it trains readers gradually into a truth that would otherwise cause their brain to "giggle" in helpless paralysis. As Dickinson puts it,

> Tell all the truth but tell it slant -
> Success in Circuit lies
> Too bright for our infirm Delight
> The Truth's superb surprise
>
> As Lightning to the Children eased
> With explanation kind
> The Truth must dazzle gradually
> Or every man be blind -

Riddles and metaphors are both tropes: non-literal or indirect modes of description. What about poetry's metrical and aural schemes? Where Aumann links Dickinson's distortion of traditional hymn scheme to her conflicted relationship to Puritan doctrine, Hills argues more broadly that it "constitutes a self-questioning, self-correcting, self-censoring mode of attention," one which is also reflected in her highly distinctive use of hyphens. Rhythmically, by echoing traditional hymns, Dickinson doesn't merely suggest, but makes us feel the familiarity of her subject, even before we know what that subject actually is. But for that same reason, when the steady rhythm stumbles, the subject itself is also rendered alien. Similarly, the sonic similarities of slanting rhymes provide clues to the riddle poem's solution; but the slant's dissonance also "sours" those associations, reminding us of substantive disparities between the denoted objects. In both cases, Hills argues, the form engenders a feeling of orientation and safety which is then unsettled by being twisted. A prose format would miss out on both aspects of this dynamic.

Hills's discussion focuses most directly on Dickinson's use of poetic devices to enact a heuristic process for the reader. Like Hills, *Eileen John* attends closely to Dickinson's use of specific formal devices. But at the same time, like Furtak and Ostas, she emphasizes the poet's use of those devices as tools for her own epistemic purposes, specifically in seeking to understand aspects of the world for which no stable subsuming perspective can be achieved.

Substantively, John argues that Dickinson embraces a processual model of knowledge highly consonant with those proposed by Furtak and Ostas. Where traditional static accounts treat knowledge as a state of an agent achieved by standing in a privileged relation to a proposition, Furtak, Ostas, and John take Dickinson to offer a model of knowledge as an ongoing process of getting a grip on an overflowingly complex reality using limited perceptual and cognitive resources that include bodily feeling and emotion. John further connects this view to the development of expertise or know-how, especially within the context of domestic labor. Thus, in

We play at Paste -
Till qualified, for Pearl -

the poet suggests that while we are tempted to dismiss activities like making pretend gems as mere play, such practice actually develops genuine practical skills. The same goes by implication, John argues, for the higher-order epistemic skill of distinguishing mere appearance from genuine value, especially as it applies to determining which of our own activities are genuinely skillful. In each case, although the transition from ignorance to ability involves a degree and depth of difference that tempts us to "deem" our previous selves "a fool," there is also deep continuity in the skills involved. By extension, we can add, although we might be tempted to dismiss poetry as mere play, the skills of observation, distinction, and feeling it cultivates function not just as proxies for, but as practice in and even instances of genuine epistemic ability.

Formally, John traces out the model of knowledge as an ongoing process of skillful but inevitably incomplete achievement through a pair of metaphoric images: hinges and seams. She takes a hinge, as a mechanism that allows one to swing between distinct planes, to be an apt figure for Dickinson's conviction that "there are radically different kinds of thought, that a human being is not in a position to work with only one of them, and can move between them with some competence." Thus, in

> The Missing All - prevented Me
> From missing minor Things.
> If nothing larger than a World's
> Departure from a Hinge -
> Or Sun's extinction, be observed -
> 'Twas not so large that I
> Could lift my Forehead from my work
> For Curiosity.

the World swings out of view as the poet remains engaged in quotidian labor such as needlework. Here again, we find the poet seeking, and failing to find, the sort of positive hold on the global "All" sought by philosophers, dogmatists, and skeptics alike. But at the same time, John argues, this absence is not devastating: the poet is confident that "there are other things worth not missing, and we are capable of not missing them, within the absorbing work . . . at hand."

John's other focal image is the seam, deployed most systematically in "Don't put up my Thread and Needle," in which Dickinson describes falling asleep at her needlework, with her sight and her performance becoming increasingly "crooked" even as she dreams she is sewing fine, straight hems. In this poem, unlike "We Play at Paste," the poet displays confidence in herself as a "competent, discerning agent," in both practical and epistemic senses; the problem is that she is temporarily unable to implement those abilities because exhaustion has put her out of touch with her work—much as a change of Mood can render her unable to recognize God in nature, or to embrace phenomenal states as her own.

A seam, like a hinge, is a familiar, functional feature of daily domestic life, specifically one that creates a strong yet flexible connection between two things while leaving them different. John's argument is not that Dickinson is especially prone to employ hinges and seams as metaphors for knowledge. Rather, she claims that when these images do appear in Dickinson's poems, they articulate a model of knowledge that the poet often also expresses in other terms and endorses more generally. In particular, as we have seen, Dickinson frequently oscillates between the close observation of local, familiar phenomena and values, especially those embedded in domestic life, and the search for a more cosmic, impersonal, abstract perspective— a search which inevitably fails to discover a positive "All" distinct from lived experience, but which does not therefore conclude that all there really is a void or a bare physical substrate.

John's argument is also not just that Dickinson sometimes employs hinges and seams as tropes to describe an epistemic state she finds interesting. Rather, she argues that formally, Dickinson frequently employs words themselves as hinges and seams, or "pivoting points": devices that aptly join two perspectives or systems of thought while leaving them distinct. The typical mechanism of juncture is that of the pun: for instance, in "Don't put up my Thread and Needle" Dickinson plays on the sonic similarities between "seam" and "seem," and between "sew" and the multiple meanings of "so." Although the association between punning homophones is clearly arbitrary—we are palpably aware that their semantic values are distinct—the sonic similarity links those values in our minds, sets us up to seek out more substantive similarities, and makes them especially satisfying once found.

Thus, much as with her distinctive use of hyphens and of hymn scheme, Dickinson's use of puns as "pivoting points" between incommensurable perspectives provides her with an efficient mechanism for articulating the sorts of complex relations among disparate thoughts that she is especially invested in expressing. Any articulation of her intended contents using more standard logical, causal, or other connectives would be too coarse-grained and determinate to capture the open-ended, multi-dimensional relations that Dickinson takes to obtain between the disparate perspectives she wants to stage. In this sense, Dickinson needs such hinge words to place "planes of thought" into relations that are "precise and yet somehow free," in a phrase John appropriates from Ted Hughes.[8]

Perhaps, given sufficient effort and ingenuity, this complex network of relations could be articulated in ordinary prose. However, such a prose paraphrase would still fail to enact the patterns of connection that Dickinson's poems do. And as such, it would also fail to accomplish a crucial part of the task those poems perform: of enabling her readers to trace out those patterns for themselves, by giving them direct, experiential access to their performance. Moreover, it is plausible that enacting such patterns itself has a substantive justificatory

8. Hughes, "Introduction to A Choice of Emily Dickinson's Verse," 359; cited in John, ch. 6 of this volume.

function. First, it inculcates through practice a distinctive species of know-how: a "mode of attention" for navigating among and interpreting certain types of phenomena. In themselves, the resulting cognitive traits might not be epistemically valuable. However, if we take knowledge to be the achievement of a certain kind of acknowledgment of and reconciliation with seemingly recalcitrant phenomena, as Dickinson arguably does, then it becomes more plausible that such cognitive know-how is epistemically relevant. Further, by demonstrating how to achieve that goal in a series of particular cases—some of which, like riddles about hummingbirds, are amusing; others of which, like metaphors about death, are potentially horrifying—it also trains the reader to accomplish that goal in other cases, for themselves.

The operative question, of course, is whether techniques of pun, metaphor, rhythm and rhyme, do reliably conduce to knowledge at least in the sense of getting a robust grip on the world, or instead produce a dangerous simulacrum of reason. The worry that rhetorical devices seduce readers into epistemic complacency is both longstanding and well-placed. However, while the particular structures are quite different from those employed in standard philosophical practice, the idea that formal structures have justificatory status because they display, and thereby prompt readers to enact, certain trains of thought is not especially alien; indeed it constitutes a core intuition about the nature of proof. Moreover, both Hills and John argue that Dickinson deploys these techniques in a way that brings them significantly closer to philosophy. In her hands, these formal techniques function, not to lull readers into comfortable streams of association, but rather as prompts to scrutinize and analyze first-order external and internal phenomena to which the reader has evidential access. More importantly, Dickinson also characteristically probes her own trains of thought, so that the "precise and yet somehow free relations" that are expressed by what Hills calls Dickinson's "argument-making metrical resources" are themselves called into critical question, qualified, and sometimes rejected altogether. The "proofs" given by Dickinson's poems cannot provide indubitable signs of verity. But for a particular, limited agent grappling with how best to stitch together a comprehensive, authentic understanding of an overwhelmingly complex reality, as Dickinson is, and as many of us are, they provide a productive set of tools and products—ones that her readers must then put to the test for themselves.

WHY DICKINSON FOR PHILOSOPHY?

Stepping back from the specific contributions of our particular authors, what can we now say about the relevance of Dickinson for philosophy, given the overall picture of her poetry that has emerged? We've canvassed Dickinson's take on philosophical topics such as the ontological status of God, sound, the self, and the nature and basis of knowledge. We've also seen something about how and why she deploys distinctively poetic techniques to express contents and per-suade her readers, including herself. But in the absence of an anteced-ent interest in Dickinson, why should philosophers care about what she says and does?

First, Dickinson demonstrates a suite of productive epistemic practices that complement standard philosophical techniques of analysis and inference. We can work toward knowing by allocating attention to particular familiar but puzzling phenomena which we encounter within ourselves and in the world around us; by trying on multiple, contrasting interpretations of those phenomena that link them to other situations and scenarios; by probing our intuitive and evaluative responses to them under those interpretations, to see if we can affirm them as belonging to our reality; and by attempting to reconcile, or at least find ways to navigate effectively among, the resulting interpretations. And we can treat this epistemic work as a kind of ongoing, quotidian labor, one that is often bound up with the practical tasks of everyday life but that also roams to remote corners of modal space.

We should expect this work to require sustained attention, courage, and fortitude. We should acknowledge that it will never be finished, because we are constantly encountering new phenomena, and because those phenomena are too complex to be susceptible to any single, fully reconciled accounting. Sometimes we are stymied: our "Strings are Snapt, [our] Bow - to Atoms blown - "; we face a "blank" of pain or a "cleaving" of alienation that our brain can only "giggle" at, agog. When that happens, it is profoundly terrible. In that case, the best we can do—the only thing to do if we are to remain alive—is to get up the next morning and set ourselves back to work, mending those strings, sewing seams of partial comprehension, and learning again to wonder at the world within and around us.

Second, contra the stereotype of a reclusive poet confined to her Amherst drawing room and garden, Dickinson often appears to be engaged in this epistemic labor with others, both by appropriating other thinkers' perspectives and claims, and also by inviting her readers to observe and interpret structurally analogous phenomena for themselves. But even when she does labor on her own, this already involves a kind of conversation, in which she stages multiple personas, and she can "stun" herself by learning that she resonates to or rejects possibilities in ways she would not have expected. In either case, Dickinson demonstrates a suite of techniques for fruitful conversation that complement standard philosophical techniques of argumentation. We can entice our interlocutors to pay close attention to the relevant phenomena by employing precise, vivid descriptions of concrete instances, or else by presenting them with intriguing puzzles to solve. We can offer them "kind" initial explanations to avoid "dazzling" them into cognitive paralysis, which we replace with successively richer interpretations. And we can employ expressions and forms that are consistent with and reinforce the broader perspectives being presented, and that in some cases actually exemplify the contents being expressed. Poetry is not philosophy. One of its constitutive aims is to please, at least in the ecumenical sense of eliciting admiration at the aptness of how it accomplishes what it sets out to do. But this aim is not incompatible with engaging in a serious, self-critical attempt to make sense of the world, and oneself, and one's place in the world. Writing and reading poetry can be a mode of philosophizing, one that affords epistemic payoffs not attainable via "straight" analysis and inference. In that practice, Dickinson shows us a way.[9]

REFERENCES

Adorno, Theodor. "Commitment." *New Left Review* 1, no. 87–88 (1974): 78.

Bacon, Francis. *The Advancement of Learning*. 1st Paul Dry Books Edition. Edited by G. W. Kitchin. Philadelphia: Paul Dry Books, 2000.

Chalmers, David. *Constructing the World*. Oxford: Oxford University Press, 2012.

Erfani, Farhang. "Dickinson and Sartre on Facing the Brutality of Brute Existence." In *Emily Dickinson and Philosophy*, edited by Jed Deppman et al., 175–187. Cambridge: Cambridge University Press, 2013.

Hartman, Geoffrey. "Language from the Point of View of Literature." In *Beyond Formalism: Literary Essays 1958–1970*. New Haven: Yale University Press, 1970.

9. Thanks to Richard Eldridge for the initial invitation to produce this volume and for sage advice and substantive philosophical feedback throughout. Thanks to the departments of English and Philosophy and the Center for Cultural Analysis at Rutgers University for sponsoring a workshop at which many of these papers were first presented, and to workshop participants including especially Avi Alpert, Ernie Lepore, Colin Jager, Doug Jones, Jonah Siegel, and Abigail Zitin. Thanks above all to the contributors, for their insightful readings of Dickinson and their incisive and sympathetic feedback on each others' papers.

Hughes, Ted. 2002. "Introduction to *A Choice of Emily Dickinson's Verse*." In *Emily Dickinson: Critical Assessments*, vol. 2, edited by Graham Clarke, 355–359. Mountfield, East Sussex: Helm Information.

Nussbaum, Martha. "Form and Content, Philosophy and Literature." In *Love's Knowledge: Love's Knowledge: Essays on Philosophy and Literature*. Oxford: Oxford University Press, 1992.

Chapter 1

Forms of Emotional Knowing and Unknowing

Skepticism and Belief in Dickinson's Poetry

RICK ANTHONY FURTAK

How are the allure of truth, and the problem or challenge of attaining knowledge, addressed in Emily Dickinson's poetry? Continually at issue in her verse are the possibilities and limits of knowing the nature of the surrounding world, including the minds of others. Many of Dickinson's poems give voice to wonder, frustration, and the feeling of illumination or insight, along with other emotional states involved in exploring the promise of knowledge and confronting skeptical questions. This chapter will focus especially on moments in Dickinson's poetry at which an encounter with the natural or human world is portrayed as moving the poet toward either an intensification or a partial resolution of doubt—a dialectic through which she, the implied speaker, articulates the affective struggle to make sense of the world and to find herself at home in it. As we shall see, the philosophical thinking that unfolds in her lyrics is often preoccupied with a characteristic human distress about our finite limitations *and* with a contrary,

The Poetry of Emily Dickinson. Elisabeth Camp, Oxford University Press (2021). © Oxford University Press.
DOI: 10.1093/oso/9780190651190.003.0002

but intimately related, longing to be reconciled with our finitude. I will be attentive throughout this essay to the ways in which Dickinson's metrical techniques are pertinent to her investigation of these themes.

Let me begin by analyzing a poem of three quatrains, in Dickinson's typical ballad measure (with just a few departures from this pattern). Here, the prevailing attitude is in harmony with Emerson's claim that, in the natural world, one can find a "sanctity which shames our religions,"[1] as the poet speaks about a day of sacred observance—spent not in attending Mass, but in being receptive to what surrounds her while she is outdoors within her own yard.

> Some keep the Sabbath going to Church -
> I keep it, staying at Home -
> With a Bobolink for a Chorister -
> And an Orchard, for a Dome -
>
> Some keep the Sabbath in Surplice -
> I just wear my Wings -
> And instead of tolling the Bell, for Church,
> Our little Sexton - sings.
>
> God preaches, a noted Clergyman -
> And the sermon is never long,
> So instead of getting to Heaven, at last -
> I'm going, all along.
>
> (Fr 236, J 324; 1861)

The speaker is portraying a day of worship in her orchard, with natural replacements for every aspect of a traditional church service. Dickinson's poem manifests a preference for finding God in nature, in

---

1. Emerson, "Nature," from *Essays: Second Series*, in *The Essential Writings of Ralph Waldo Emerson*, 364.

a way that allows her to be at home in the world and to experience it as meaningful—without looking beyond this life to an otherworldly realm of meaning. A series of similar low vowel sounds throughout the poem—"going," "Bobolink," "Chorister," "Orchard," "Dome," "tolling," "noted," and again "going"—resonate with the last word in the second line, "Home." The harmonious pattern of assonance, echoing off the long *O* in *home*, indicates what the poem plainly conveys: that the speaker feels happily contented, by virtue of her attunement to the natural environment in this familiar place. Although she is out of step with the churchgoers in her human community, that is only because she is hearing a different drummer. And she appears to be at peace, having traded conventional priestly vestments (or "Surplice") for her own humble "Wings," and the church's "Dome" for the overhead branches of her "Orchard." Rather than listening to hymns sung by a choir, she hears the ebullient sounds of a native songbird, whose name ("Bobolink") is an onomatopoetic imitation of its warbling chirp. Instead of hearing a "noted" clergyman such as might be found in a church, one who is *noted* in the sense of having achieved prestige among mortals, the speaker enjoys the actual *notes* of birdsong. Natural value, directly perceived, replaces the socially coordinated meanings of institutional religion. Yet this poem speaks from a perspective that is too reverent to be appropriately called "secular": it expresses a natural piety. For the poet in her orchard, what is spoken *about* in a pastor's long sermon (lines 9–10) is immediately present as a fact of experience, available to those who have ears to hear and eyes to see. It is not a postulated paradise described from afar.

In the final two lines, the speaker of Dickinson's poem expresses in her own words a version of Thoreau's belief that "Here or nowhere is our heaven."[2] While their New England neighbors are praying to reach Heaven "at last," in a realm beyond life on Earth,

---

2. Thoreau, *A Week on the Concord and Merrimack Rivers*, 380.

these authors—one might say—are "already there, in a natural heaven."[3] Taking poetic flight while her feet remain firmly on the ground, she affirms that it is possible to have an intimate acquaintance with the divine within Nature. As she remarks in line 6, "I just [i.e., merely] wear my Wings"—as if this kind of knowledge really does seem, at times, easy to obtain. On the whole, what comes to voice in this poem is a sense that the moment from which the poet speaks is one when it truly seems that "Heaven is under our feet as well as over our heads."[4] Why, then, does she proceed to comment that she is "going, all along" to heaven (lines 11–12)—on her way, rather than already there? Why should this poem of natural piety and wonder end on a contrary emotional note, by mentioning a goal unattained? One plausible interpretation of its closing lines is that they qualify what would otherwise be an immoderate statement of blissful communion with one's natural surroundings. The speaker is *almost* carried away into declaring presumptuously that she has now arrived without remainder in an earthly heaven—yet she is careful to stop short of doing so. Furthermore, if what is sacred is to be found here in this world, then heaven should no longer be conceptualized as a goal at which one arrives if and when, after mortal life has ended, one is given an entrance ticket to the afterlife as a reward. Instead, to lead *this* life as if we were already in heaven requires that we be always in the process of inhabiting the finite world in such a way that we are able to find joy in every moment.[5] As long as a person exists, this process will never be finished: it remains constantly ongoing. We might occasionally wish

---

3. Vendler, *Dickinson*, 73. Vendler is describing Dickinson only, not Thoreau, but the description fits him as well.

4. Thoreau, *Walden*, 276.

5. In this sense, we see in Dickinson's poem what Abrams has called "the celebration of that which lives, moves, and evolves . . . over whatever is lifeless, inert, and unchanging" (*Natural Supernaturalism*, 431–432).

not to remain forever unfinished, and to reach a terminus where everything is complete, but we also have reason to be distrustful of this wish. The desire to reach a conclusive endpoint, where we *are* finished, is a longing to be liberated from the realm of time and change—the realm of becoming in which we human beings exist. It is therefore a yearning to free ourselves altogether from the limits of the human condition. At the end of "Some keep the Sabbath going to Church," Dickinson considers yet rejects this understandable longing—in favor of being at home in the world, as much as she *can* be, and knowing it as a holy place.

Yet the world neither evidently nor always appears to be so glorious.[6] And Dickinson is not facile about the task of finding one's everyday surroundings deserving of such hymns of praise as are heard in churches, worthy of such religious emotions as wonder and reverence. Accordingly, other poems speak in an affective register of being estranged and feeling ill at ease. The first stanza of J 413, for instance, is a lamentation of finding oneself chronically *out* of place, here in this world and presumably elsewhere:

> I never felt at Home - Below -
> And in the Handsome Skies
> I shall not feel at Home - I know -
> I don't like Paradise -

(Fr 437, J 413; 1862)

The predominant mood expressed by the speaker is one of such profound alienation that all memory or expectation of at-home-ness is eliminated: being in harmony with one's surroundings, or finding *any*

---

6. To demonstrate that—despite all evidence to the contrary—existence *can* be, and seem, glorious is a major aim of Rilke's *Duino Elegies*—as is cogently argued by James D. Reid in *Being Here Is Glorious: On Rilke, Poetry, and Philosophy*.

kind of comprehensible meaning in them, seems unimaginable and thus impossible. This estrangement sets into relief as precarious, and sometimes unavailable, the state of mind in which one can honestly rejoice at how the world seems, in which Heaven is felt to be present in one's surroundings and under one's feet. But Nature also surprises. If Dickinson in "Some keep the Sabbath going to Church" is depicting a religious observance which is *partly* orchestrated by the observer— someone who perceives a heavenly significance in the world around her, yet partially by virtue of her own creative imagination—then the poem below ends up speaking even more decidedly in the voice of an axiological realist, one whose encounter with a world enchanted with value overflows what she herself anticipates at the outset:

My period had come for Prayer -
No other Art - would do -
My Tactics missed a rudiment -
Creator - Was it you?

God grows above - so those who pray
Horizons - must ascend -
And so I stepped upon the North
To see this Curious Friend -

His House was not - no sign had He -
By Chimney - or by Door
Could I infer his Residence -
Vast Prairies of Air

Unbroken by a Settler -
Were all that I could see -
Infinitude - Had'st Thou no Face
That I might look on Thee?

The Silence condescended -
Creation stopped - for Me -

But awed beyond my errand -
I worshipped - did not "pray" -

(Fr 525, J 564, 1863)

Prayer is introduced in the first stanza as an "Art" involving "Tactics," a deliberate practice intended to bring about a pious, reverent outlook suited for communicating with the divine. To pray in this manner is to be an agent enacting a certain purpose: the speaker knows what she is seeking, as well as where to look for it. Because God is conventionally envisioned as dwelling "above," lines 5–6 inform us that those who pray must lift up their eyes and look above the horizon. Reasonably enough, for Dickinson the horizon signifies "the point of fusion of this world and the next,"[7] so all of the strategies that the speaker has described so far reflect sound judgment on the part of a person setting out to pray. Facing or mounting northward also makes sense, to adopt another culturally standard habit of thought: as God is *above*, so also north is *up*, though not for any reason grounded in the nature of things.

Gazing out into the world with a specific plan, the speaker feels disconcerted when she finds no distinct "sign" from which she can "infer" the presence of divinity. She spends much of the third and fourth stanzas naming the sort of evidence she seeks, based on her preconceived notions about what it must be like to find God in nature: a "House" with "Chimney" or "Door," perhaps, or *some* sign that he resides there in the clouds. Or a "Face," maybe? She finds none of these, but only "Vast Prairies of Air / Unbroken by a Settler" (lines 12–13), and is initially disappointed that her search has turned up empty. Hoping to find a door, she has discovered only air, and the slant rhyme of "Door"/"Air"—the poem's first imperfect rhyme— imitates her jarring response, upon failing to meet with the type of sign she had expected. How can she pray, she asks, when "all" that she

---

7. Farr, *The Passion of Emily Dickinson*, 90–91.

can see is broad unmarked space, no evident boundary such as the threshold of a house? Then, as if lingering over the expansive vowel sounds in that phrase, "Vast Prairies of Air," the speaker is struck by the impression that perhaps "Infinitude"—one of her own names for God—does not correspond to the parochial and anthropomorphic preconceptions with which she began. *This* is when she is astonished by the realization that she has in fact discovered something after all—something not of her making, and not measurable by her most readily available concepts of the divine. Although not an initially recognizable sign, it is significant beyond what she had at first dreamt of encountering, evoking in her the religious emotion of awe and the religious attitude of worship. Her own horizons of expectancy have now been surpassed, as in lines 19–20 she is "awed beyond [her] errand" and falls figuratively to her knees in adoration. What she has found in the immense skies and the "Silence" holds greater meaning than what she had sought when she went out to "pray"—a term now placed in scare quotes, so meager is what it initially meant compared with the potent mode of worship she has found. As the poet writes in an 1863 letter, "I was thinking to-day . . . that the 'supernatural' was only the natural disclosed."[8] On these terms, something true has been disclosed or made known in "My period had come for Prayer," which the speaker finds utterly amazing.

Yet is Dickinson's narrator also rejoicing? The experience of natural supernaturalism conveyed in "My period had come for Prayer" differs from the contented joyfulness found in "Some keep the Sabbath going to Church," though both poems ultimately identify this world as a place in which sacred radiance (or intimations of it) can be found. The mood of the speaker who is "awed beyond [her] errand" is a terrible wonder that she finds strangely exhilarating, and part of what

---

8. See *Letters of Emily Dickinson*, 260. In the same letter, Dickinson illustrates her point with the lines: "Not 'Revelation' 'tis that waits, / But our unfurnished eyes."

the poem captures (or points toward) is a sense of greater mystery. Nature has a face, with an expression that appears sometimes blank, at times benign, and which contains a mind of its own. That this mind is "other" is clear, I think, in the closing lines of "My period had come for Prayer." It is also evident in Dickinson's poem J 627, where one stanza begins by referring to "The eager look - on Landscapes - / As if they just repressed / Some Secret" (Fr 696, 1863; lines 13–15). These poems speculate that the nonhuman world may be *minded*, and that the unknown mind it harbors nonetheless provides us with hints about its existence and perhaps its character. What is it that the poet, or her first-person speaker, reports having glimpsed about this other mind? At the end of "My period had come for Prayer," it's difficult to specify what exactly has been revealed. Yet a poem can suggest, without making lucid univocal statements, asserting theses, or elaborating in further detail—and this is particularly true of Dickinson's compact and cryptic lines. An abruptly punctuated, metrically exact line of poetry can divulge or signal a truth that escapes being contained in a more prosaic statement, or that would dissolve if spelled out at length in sprawling lines of free verse. About an experience that is difficult to articulate, formal technique allows the poet to bring *something* to voice. Dickinson, at the end of "My period had come for Prayer," speaks with musical precision about an emotional state of being moved with an enigmatic spiritual insight. Something is encountered there in the vast sky: not what her religious framework has prepared her to expect, yet wondrous and awe-inspiring. She imparts the conviction that the world is significant, in ways that we can fleetingly discern if never entirely grasp.

* * *

So far, we have encountered quite variant moods or perspectives in Dickinson's poetry: those of inhabiting a tranquil heavenly Eden, in which everything we look upon is blessed with divine radiance; and of being shocked by the frightening sublime, in which awestruck silence surprisingly drowns out the effort to pray. Yet both the point of view expressed in "Some keep the Sabbath going to Church" and the one at which we arrive by the end of "My period had come for Prayer," as I have argued, present us with what is experienced as the perception of divinity in the natural world. "It is a faint intimation," as Thoreau writes, with his own gnomic suggestiveness, "yet so are the first streaks of morning."[9] But when we consider Dickinson's poems that exhibit a feeling of alienation, an uncanny failure or inability to be at home in our surroundings—where, as in line 1 of poem J 1096, she speaks of being "Strangers, in a foreign World"—we face the question of whether our perceptions can be trusted during the more seemingly enchanted moments (Fr 805, 1864). Is God perhaps only "something we project upon the blank canopy of the heavens"?[10] When, for instance, the poet says that "Creation stopped - for Me," the *for me* could be parsed as meaning "as far as I could see," or "as it seemed from my vantage point," implying that it might not *really* have stopped. While in the grip of a powerful emotion such as reverent wonder, a person may "at times be so far deluded, as to mistake the tumultuous sensations of his nerves . . . as parts or symbols of the truths which were opening on [her or] him," Coleridge warns, adding that, "during the act of knowledge itself, the objective and subjective are so instantly united" that one "cannot determine to which of the two the priority belongs."[11] This distinctly post-Kantian problem is brought up overtly in the Dickinson poem to which we now turn:

> To hear an Oriole sing
> May be a common thing -
> Or only a divine.

9. Thoreau, *Walden*, 208–209.
10. Lundin, *Emily Dickinson and the Art of Belief*, 146–147.
11. Coleridge, *Biographia Literaria*, 1: 96–98 & 1: 174–175.

It is not of the Bird
Who sings the same, unheard,
As unto Crowd -

The Fashion of the Ear
Attireth that it hear
In Dun, or fair -

So whether it be Rune,
Or whether it be none
Is of within.

The "Tune is in the Tree - "
The Skeptic - showeth me -
"No Sir! In Thee!"

(Fr 402, J 526; 1862)

"The Skeptic" is apparently the figure who insists that the tune of an Oriole's song is *not* in the objective world but only in the subject. Skeptical, this claim is, because it calls into doubt the reality of the bird's song—as beautiful, or even audible, apart from the subject who hears it. If "human consciousness participates in creating the perceptual world," or (in other words) if "our minds help to make up nature," then maybe sound or music is only conferred upon the world by us.[12] If so, then the warbling call of the Oriole would be just a projection, and not something genuinely apprehended.

Because the middle stanza of the poem asserts at face value that *whether* the bird's song seems "Dun, or fair," dull or charming, depends on how it is *attired* or clothed by the "Fashion of the Ear," some readings of this poem construe it as emphasizing a division

---

12. Lee, "Dickinson's Superb Surprise," 51.

between the human mind and the external world. Laying stress on "the gap between us and nature," the poem would on this view be affirming the supposition "that it is we who confer meaning upon the world."[13] Sound and music would, then, be *not* "in the Tree" where the bird sings ("out there," so to speak), but *merely* within the subject: "In Thee," as "the Skeptic" tells us (lines 13–15). This is what external-world skepticism encourages us to believe: that a bird's song lies in the human mind alone, rather than in the non-human world. And "To hear an Oriole sing" may seem to endorse the notion that, as Rorty states, "truth is made rather than found."[14] A more careful interpretive stance to take, I think, is to grant that the poem raises the question of *whether* this is the case without claiming to have settled it. Dickinson's letters repeatedly demonstrate her acquaintance with the ways in which our own disposition influences how the world seems—sickness darkens our day, whereas we can be elevated and made aware of "celestial things" by such a mundane fact as hearing birds sing[15]—as well as the philosophical quandary about how, in light of this, we can distinguish how things *are* from how they *seem*. Moreover, other poems observe that one's "Mood" can dictate the value, for good or bad, of the mind-independent world: "The Inner - paints the Outer," Dickinson claims in J 451, and "The Outer - from the Inner / Derives its Magnitude - / 'Tis Duke, or Dwarf, according / As is the Central Mood" (Fr 450, 1862; lines 9, 1–4). Since we have also witnessed moments in her poetry that make it sound as if significant features of the world can legitimately be revealed through our affective experience, we should hesitate to conclude that Dickinson opts for the anti-realist side of the dichotomy between *yes, the tune is in the world* and *no, it is merely in oneself*.

---

13. See, e.g., Erfani, "Dickinson and Sartre on Facing the Brutality of Brute Existence," 184–185.
14. Richard Rorty, *Contingency, Irony, and Solidarity*, 6–7.
15. See, e.g., *Letters of Emily Dickinson*, 40 & 331–332.

She is more philosophically sophisticated than this. Dickinson acknowledges that one's way of seeing conditions how the world appears, but that this does not render illusory the beauty or meaning that we perceive. The song of the oriole, along with a receptive or appreciative listener, are both necessary conditions, and jointly sufficient, for the tune to be heard. This makes either "mind as mirror" *or* "mind as projector" analogies seem inadequate. In agreement with Emerson, Dickinson observes that we have access to the world only through our moods; in the spirit of Thoreau, she is attentive to the fact that we can shape "the very atmosphere and medium through which we look," and by altering our perspective (for example, by awakening our senses and training our aesthetic sensibility) we can thereby "affect the quality of the day."[16] Our surrounding world, then, is always viewed from our standpoint while remaining beyond us as a partially unknown reality.

Returning to this specific fifteen-line poem, "To hear an Oriole sing," we find in the second tercet the assertion that whether the bird's song is heard or unheard is *not* an indifferent matter. Metaphysically, there is a distinction between what is merely aud*ible* and what actually impinges on a listener—however, this difference is not "of the Bird," who "sings the same" in either case (lines 4–5). The sound made by the bird in the tree is in one sense empirically *there* even when entirely unheard, or heard "only" by a "divine" being yet by no "common" mortal (lines 2–3): could it be that this tune is being perceived only by an infinite mind, such as Berkeley's God, as the first tercet appears to propose? The fourth stanza elaborates that "whether

16. Thoreau, *Walden*, 87. On life as a "succession" and "flux" of moods, see Emerson, "Experience," in *Essays and Lectures*, 471–492. On these Thoreauvian and Emersonian themes, see respectively my "The Value of Being: Thoreau on Appreciating the Beauty of the World," and Stanley Cavell's, "Thinking of Emerson." Whether "well beloved or warily distrusted," for Dickinson "nature is [always] unknown," as James McIntosh observes in *Nimble Believing*, 143–145.

it be Rune, / Or whether it be none / Is of within." Because a rune is a symbol of mysterious or magical significance, what is at issue here is whether the bird's song *is* enchanting *or* value-neutral, when it is heard by a human being. To perceive things as beautiful or meaningful, Dickinson's poem attests, we must be receptive to their beauty or meaning, rather than allowing it to be lost on us. By a person with the capacity to hear, the musical quality of the oriole's vocalizations may nevertheless remain undetected, if he is unreceptive—by virtue of being distracted, of simply not listening. As one critic remarks, Dickinson's question in this poem "is not whether the ear hears; it is whether it hears a *tune*. It is about the fashion or mode or mood of the ear."[17] This suggests that the "Skeptic" in "To hear an Oriole sing" is poorly attuned to his or her surroundings, and dismisses the tune as "merely" in the observer's ear for this reason, while the person who *does* hear the beauty of the song is better in touch with the world. For the latter, the one who hears the tune, this perceptual experience *might* carry enough weight to nullify the skeptic's question. Yet the naïve realist's opinion that something like a song exists objectively "in itself," without reference to *any* observer (whether "common" or "divine"), has also been invalidated by the end of the poem.

In Carlyle's *Sartor Resartus*, we read that a "man who cannot wonder, who does not habitually wonder (and worship), is but a Pair of Spectacles behind which there is no Eye."[18] On balance, Dickinson tends to favor a comparable view, and also to be in agreement with Thoreau's claim that there is "as much beauty visible to us" in the world "as we are prepared to appreciate," but "not a grain more."[19] In lines 1–2 of poem J 1195, she cautiously affirms that "What we see we

---

17. Benfey, *Emily Dickinson and the Problem of Others*, 20–23. Emphasis in original.
18. Carlyle, *Sartor Resartus*, 54.
19. Entry dated November 4, 1858, from *The Journal of Henry D. Thoreau*. See also the entry dated August 1, 1860, in which Thoreau laments: "How much of beauty . . . on which our eyes daily rest goes unperceived by us."

know somewhat / Be it but a little" (Fr 1272, 1872). With a similar caution, I concur with Maurice Lee's assertions that, for Dickinson, "the small steps of experience" do lead at least "to partial and provisional knowledge," and that her work approaches the reality and value of the "object world" with "committed, if provisional, realism,"[20] while also placing great weight on what the subject contributes to experience. In other words, while it sustains a powerful recognition of what another author calls "the mystery of subject-object coalescence and interpenetration" in our ordinary "empirical perception," Dickinson's poetry allows the "given world" to appear "extrinsic to, and greater than, herself"[21]—as we have already seen, in our analyses of "Some keep the Sabbath going to Church" and "My period had come for Prayer." Refusing to see knowledge as a matter of invention *rather* than discovery, or Being as *merely* a construction or projection, Dickinson's work testifies to the fact that our mind is "creative and responsive at one and the same time"—it rejects the assumption that some elements of our experience simply mirror "the way things are" while others are just human fabrications.[22] In the meeting of mind and world, both the subject and the object make essential contributions, so both of these voices are allowed to register in "To hear an Oriole sing."

"But nature is a stranger yet," as Dickinson reminds us (Fr 1433, J 1400; 1877; line 17); and, in lines 15–16 of J 451 (Fr 450, 1862), she writes: "The Star's whole Secret . . . / Eyes were not meant to

---

20. Lee, *Uncertain Chances*, 173–174 & 156–157. Lee elsewhere makes the point this way: "Dickinson neither asserts absolute truths nor capitulates to a full-blown skepticism" ("Dickinson's Superb Surprise," 46–47).

21. Brantley, *Experience and Faith: The Late-Romantic Imagination of Emily Dickinson*, 76.

22. See Larmore, *The Romantic Legacy*, 28–31. He is speaking in general about insights that need to be recovered in the post-Romantic age. See also Deppman, *Trying to Think with Emily Dickinson*, 107–108: for similar reasons to my own, he claims that Dickinson respects the limits of reason outlined in Kant's *Critique of Pure Reason* "more faithfully than do Schiller, Fichte, Coleridge, or Emerson."

know." When emphasis is placed on the limits of knowledge, as it is at these and other moments in her poetry, she seems to strike an Emersonian chord. "The stars awaken a certain reverence," as he observes, "because though always present, they are inaccessible."[23] Although " 'Nature' is what we see," and "what we hear," according to poem J 668, it is also something beyond our immediate awareness: "Nature is what we know - / Yet have no art to say" (Fr 721, 1863; lines 1, 5, 9–10). Elsewhere—in poem J 797, lines 24–25— she evinces confidence that "Apprehensions - are God's introductions - / To be hallowed - accordingly," indicating trust once again that we can meet with and know something actual through our perceptual experience (Fr 849, 1864). The finitude of our predicament and of our modes of knowing are not *only* deplorable limits but also enabling conditions: we can, after all, "know somewhat" what we perceive. This "willingness to forego certainty and knowledge," *accepting* the limitations of the human standpoint,[24] often vies in Dickinson's work with the wish to know the world more completely and *not* to be reconciled to our finite limits. "This timid life of Evidence / Keeps pleading - 'I don't know,' " as the speaker of poem J 696 laments, uttering the remarkable line: "I'm finite - I can't see" (Fr 725, 1863; lines 15–16, 4). There is more to the world than the phenomena with which we have sensory acquaintance, but what *is* this "more"? Let us look at the first quatrain of J 501, a twenty-line poem—like "My period had come for Prayer"—and with an analogous rhyme scheme:

---

23. *Nature*, 1836 edition, in *The Essential Writings of Ralph Waldo Emerson*, 5. Reformulating an Aristotelian point about nature loving to hide, he adds more skeptically in "Experience" that "Nature does not like to be observed," and that our "train of moods" can function as a series of "many-colored lenses which paint the world their own hue," as "each shows only what lies in its focus." See *The Essential Writings of Ralph Waldo Emerson*, 309–311.

24. Benfey, *Emily Dickinson and the Problem of Others*, 78. Cf. Juhasz, *The Undiscovered Continent: Emily Dickinson and the Space of the Mind*, 40.

This World is not Conclusion.
A Species stands beyond -
Invisible, as Music -
But positive, as Sound -

(Fr 373, J 501; 1862)

So far, it expresses a guarded confidence that the world does not always frustrate our efforts to become acquainted with it. A phenomenon, such as the song of a bird, is empirically real ("positive, as Sound"), and it is more than a meaningless noise. Relatedly, "Music"—which is "Invisible," like sound waves themselves—is not for that reason to be undermined by skeptical arguments against its existence.[25] Following those first four lines, however, are these (lines 5–8):

It beckons, and it baffles -
Philosophy - don't know -
And through a Riddle, at the last -
Sagacity, must go -

Now Dickinson's reader is given a reminder that being is not perfectly transparent to our efforts to know and understand it. Also gesturing toward whatever "Species" of existence may transcend us, another poem stays eerily reticent: "Behind the hill is sorcery / And everything unknown" (Fr 1662, J 1603; 1884; lines 5–6). At these moments, Dickinson's lines illustrate what Sharon Cameron may have in mind when she credits the poet with recognizing that "otherness or difference is at the heart of visible presence," for instance in "the difference between the speaker and the landscape."[26] And that is not all: not only is external nature knowable by us only partially, but

25. See Kimpel, *Emily Dickinson as Philosopher*, 228–229.
26. Cameron, *Lyric Time*, 184–185.

we also carry within our own minds more than we could ever know. Poems such as J 670 allude to terrifying inward mysteries that we harbor: "One need not be a Chamber - to be Haunted - / One need not be a House - / The Brain has Corridors - surpassing / Material Place" (Fr 407, 1862; lines 1–4). According to the speaker in this poem, an "External Ghost" (line 6) is less frightening than what lies inwardly hidden, our buried emotions and unbearable memories and *all* that is unconsciously within us: "Ourself behind ourself, concealed - / Should startle most" (lines 13–14). This would include what might be called simply *the* unconscious, that in us which is "other" than us, as well as the subjective wellsprings of our own emotions. As poem J 480 wonders, how can one account for whatever unknown and unpredictable powers govern our capacity to love? Here are the first two stanzas:

"Why do I love" You, Sir?
Because -
The Wind does not require the Grass
To answer - Wherefore when He pass
She cannot keep Her place.

Because He knows - and
Do not You -
And We know not -
Enough for Us
The Wisdom it be so -

(Fr 459, 1862)

Even as the speaker in these last two lines (9–10) attempts to persuade herself that we must accept the limits of what we can explain, the poem's haltingly irregular rhythmic pattern stutters along in fitful efforts to find metaphors and occasionally to rhyme (as in lines

3–4), as if seeking rhyme *or* reason. Neither "He" the wind—who affects the grass without demanding why she, the grass, is moved—nor "You," the "Sir" who is being addressed, nor "We" human beings collectively, can entirely account for what moves us, due to the dark background out of which our emotions arise. Yet even as she acknowledges this, Dickinson betrays a restless feeling of dissatisfaction, an "irritable reaching after" explanation that still gnaws at her,[27] as if she longs to fathom the depths of her own mind while knowing that she cannot.

The poem therefore acts out, or talks through, a kind of ambivalence: its insistence that love just eludes rational comprehension competes with its wish to know more completely why one loves. It gives voice to an emotional craving for knowledge about the grounds of one's own emotions. In this sense, it reiterates the desire to be liberated from one's own finite condition with all of its limitations—in particular, the limits of what one can know—and, at the same time, it counsels against being guided by that longing. Its speaker declares herself satisfied that she cannot answer this "Why?" question—nor could anyone, for that matter—and maintains that it was inappropriately asked. Yet she is evidently unconvinced that "just because" is the only available reply, that we can talk only of causes and not of reasons here. Dickinson's poem embodies what Stanley Cavell refers to as "the ambivalence in Kant's central idea of limitation," namely "that we simultaneously crave its comfort and crave escape from its comfort, that we want . . . to be lawfully wedded to the world and at the same time illicitly intimate with it."[28] Plagued by ongoing uncertainty when we seek to understand human existence, we would like

27. In a letter to his brothers George and Tom, John Keats writes of "*Negative Capability*, that is when [a] man is capable of being in uncertainties, Mysteries, doubts, without any irritable reaching after fact & reason." See Keats, *Complete Poems and Selected Letters*, 491–492. Emphasis in original.

28. Cavell, *In Quest of the Ordinary: Lines of Skepticism and Romanticism*, 31–32.

to arrive at a totally sufficient explanation. Once again, however, wanting to reach a final and unqualified understanding is another form of the wish to "have something finished" and to escape the always-unfinished process of becoming which simply *is* the human condition.[29] As Dickinson writes in two late letters, "on subjects of which we know nothing," including "Love" as well as the thoughts of any specific person, our fate is this: "we both believe, and disbelieve a hundred times an Hour."[30] As for the aspiration toward finality, " 'It is finished' can never be said of us,"[31] and this goes for the desire to know limitlessly.

> Wonder - is not precisely Knowing
> And not precisely Knowing not -
> A beautiful but bleak condition
> He has not lived who has not felt -

(Fr 1347, J 1331; 1874)

Here, in the first stanza of poem J 1331, Dickinson locates the human being's epistemic situation, and the characteristic emotion of the philosopher, on a continuum in between the extremes of absolute knowledge and utter ignorance. Like the figure of Eros in Plato's *Symposium* (and Socrates, the philosopher who is likened to Eros in this dialogue),[32] we who feel wonder are in an intermediate place. We have enough knowledge to be aware that knowing is a

---

29. The aspiration to be "finished"—with human existence, or with one's explanation and understanding of it, is denounced throughout Kierkegaard's pseudonymous *Concluding Unscientific Postscript*.

30. From a letter dated April 1882, in *The Letters of Emily Dickinson*, ed. Johnson and Ward, 3: 728.

31. From a letter dated June 1878, in *The Letters of Emily Dickinson*, ed. Johnson and Ward, 2: 613.

32. See the chapter titled "The Definition of 'Philosopher' in Plato's *Symposium*," in Pierre Hadot's *What Is Ancient Philosophy?*, 39–51.

good thing and to aspire toward knowing more, but we do not possess it so completely as to be fully satiated in our longing to know and understand. To have never had this longing awakened, never to have felt wonder, is equated in line 4 with *not having lived*, in what sounds like an echo of Thoreau's reason for choosing a philosophical life—so that he would "not, when I came to die, discover that I had not lived."[33] Following one's sense of wonder can lead to discoveries that are "beautiful," yet this affective state is also "bleak" (line 3). Human reason is plagued by questions it cannot resist wondering about, Dickinson appears to say, but which it is frustratingly unable to resolve with certainty. Our plight is to navigate this middle region between "knowing not" and "knowing," feeling other epistemic emotions that fall somewhere between those two extremes—the aforementioned wonder and frustration, along with awe, perplexity, joyful illumination when insight is gained, disappointment at *not* being able to comprehend, and surprise—the "affective correlate" of discovering something by chance.[34] And this list could easily be extended further, to include: emotions of conjecture and surmise, terror and fear, the passions of doubt and conviction, along with astonishment, amazement, incredulity, suspicion, unfamiliarity, and calm (the feeling of being at home, instead of being unsettled).

* * *

The last poem that I shall discuss is saturated with a sense of wonder, and from start to finish it refers to emotions of knowing and

---

33. Thoreau, *Walden*, 87.
34. As surprise is described by Lee: see *Uncertain Chances*, 155–156. See also Vendler, *Dickinson*, 455–456, and, relatedly, Benfey, *Emily Dickinson and the Problem of Others*, 23–24. In a letter from 1882, in which she claims that "maturity only enhances [the sense of] mystery," Dickinson writes cryptically that "God's unique capacity is too surprising to surprise." See *Letters of Emily Dickinson*, 367–368.

unknowing. Dickinson alludes to Coleridge, the most philosophically minded poet among the English Romantics, whose 1798 poem "Frost at Midnight" begins, "The Frost performs its secret ministry." The ministry of the frost is her starting point, and it is emblematic of a subtle yet perceptible significance in the nonhuman world. Percept*ible*, that is, although often unperceived by us. Her poem hints of other minds that remain partly hidden because we do not take the trouble to notice—not merely due to the finite limits of the human intellect, beyond which lies an unknowable mystery. What is in principle within our reach, the poem insinuates, is wondrous: and it will seem this way *if* it is approached with the right kind of receptivity. A reader with enough familiarity with Dickinson's verse to expect an opening line of four-beat tetrameter—the metrical expectation that her work invites us to form—will hear an audible pause, an astonished gasp, after just *three* iambic feet in the first line announce an overnight visitor who is now (like the fourth beat) absent.

The Frost was never seen -
If met, too rapid passed,
Or in too unsubstantial Team -
The Flowers notice first

A Stranger hovering round
A Symptom of alarm
In Villages remotely set
But search effaces him

Till some retrieveless Night
Our Vigilance at waste
The Garden gets the only shot
That never could be traced.

Unproved is much we know -
Unknown the worst we fear -

Of Strangers is the Earth the Inn
Of Secrets is the Air -

To analyze perhaps
A Philip would prefer
But Labor vaster than myself
I find it to infer.

(Fr 1190, J 1202; 1870)

The "Philip" mentioned in the last stanza is the one who asks Jesus to show him the hidden God, as the sufficient proof he needs (it will "suffice," he says) and is rebuked by Christ, who asks: "Have I been so long time with you, and yet hast thou not known me?"[35] His wish to "analyze" (line 17) thus represents the demand for explanation, in the form of a purposeful assertive will that *murders to dissect*, taking a thing apart in order to know it. By contrast, to "infer" (line 20) is to gather from insufficient evidence that something is true, or that it is real—a process that may involve guesswork, speculation, and openness to faint intimations. Against the skeptical demand for proof, Dickinson's poem asks us to consider: is it not the case that, as line 13 states, "Unproved is much we know"? Or, in other words, that much (arguably most) of what we reasonably call "knowledge" is *morally certain* rather than incontrovertibly established?[36] The reason why the frost was unperceived, "never seen," was that it was

---

35. John 14: 8–9. King James translation. In what follows I allude to Wordsworth's poem "The Tables Turned," the spirit of which is very much in harmony with the Dickinson poem under discussion.

36. The term "morally certain" is used by Descartes, Hume, and Kant, among others. Following Cavell, Christopher Benfey says this: "Though we may not possess knowledge about the world, or know with certainty that [it] exists," nevertheless "we can acknowledge our nearness to and involvement with it" (*Emily Dickinson and the Problem of Others*, 65–67). "She asks us," he adds, "to renounce our demands for proof, for certainty, for possession," and (particularly in "The Frost was never seen") advises a "mood of trusting uncertainty" instead. Pages 110–113.

not met with or noticed, although there to *be* seen—after all, frost is not invisible to the human eye—or, *if* met, "too rapid passed" (lines 1–2). Some of the "Strangers" and "Secrets" which inhabit "Earth" and "Air," as lines 15–16 remind us, may lurk beyond the bounds of our comprehension—but others, like the frost, go undetected because we were unconscious, not looking, or rushing past them inattentively. As in "To hear an Oriole sing," beauty exists *in* the world to be discovered by the appreciative beholder, although it does not force itself upon us if we fail to pay attention. It is clear that the meaning of the frost is *not* lost upon other members of the natural world, such as the flowers to whom it is an alarming danger (lines 4–6)—yet it is delicate and indistinct, not as striking as the vast silent sky in "My period had come for Prayer." As in that poem, however, we must approach the world not just with preconceived notions but with a readiness to find whatever might be there. The frost (and, by extrapolation, Nature) from which we are estranged need *not* be a stranger, but could become a neighbor with whom we are well acquainted. "But search effaces him" (line 8). Analysis, demand for proof, aggressive grasping, and methodical investigation will not reveal what we seek to understand. In our own garden and on the grass is a perceptible and recognizable "other" whom we nonetheless have not acknowledged. It is not only due to our finitude that we sometimes cannot see. So the poem contains a lament about failures to see and to know, and it may also imply an imperative: that we must be receptive to discovering value in our surroundings, and permit ourselves to be surprised by what is not ourselves. We must change our way of seeing. At the same time, this poem does not simply blame the would-be perceiver of the frost (or, of the world). Much inevitably falls beyond our notice, because it is either contingently (perhaps tragically) out of our view or else wholly unknowable. The vantage point of the speaker who knows *that* the frost was there to be seen *yet* not observed by any human being sounds like that of an infinite mind, which ours is not. It seems that, contrary to some readings of Dickinson, the division between mind and world is not an insurmountable gap that bars us from knowledge;[37] indeed, it is a condition of knowing what we *can* (emotionally) know. "The Frost was never seen" is about what *happens* to fall outside of our range, and it simultaneously sounds a note of lamentation about our necessarily limited perspective.

Across Dickinson's corpus, and even within a single poem, we find widely varying and discrepant emotional attitudes: the natural world can be peacefully enchanting, or startlingly shocking; torment-ingly at a distance or estranged from us, yet at other times satisfyingly responsive or familiar. Likewise, other minds can represent bewilder-ing mysteries or sadly missed opportunities to connect, but they also provide us with inspiring (if partial) insights and render us capable of knowing. This list also could go on—even in relation to the small set of poems and fragments that I have been interpreting here—and it would include other affective antitheses. Rather than asking Dickinson to make up her mind about which way things *really* are, or deciding that she can only affirm variant truths by accepting a "princi-ple of paradoxical contradiction" which she irrationally does not care to resolve,[38] I think we should view her as making use of lyric poetry as a form in which more emotions are allowed to speak, in order to do justice to the various ways in which the world can legitimately seem to be.[39] A plurality of perspectival truths, not self-evidently capable

37. See, for example, Diehl, *Dickinson and the Romantic Imagination*, 36 & 53–54.
38. As Helen Vendler unfortunately does in her otherwise excellent chapter on Dickinson in *Poets Thinking*, 90–91.
39. Because, as we have noted, Emerson sometimes worries that our moods contradict each other, or that they veil us from the truth—see also, e.g., *Essays and Lectures*, 406 & 587— Dickinson is more in line with a famous claim made by Nietzsche, that "There is *only* a perspective seeing, *only* a perspective 'knowing'; and the *more* affects we allow to speak about one thing, the *more* eyes, different eyes, we can use to observe one thing, the more complete will our 'concept' of this thing, our 'objectivity', be" (Third Essay, Section 12, in *On the Genealogy of Morals*, 119. Emphasis in original).

of being reconciled, can each be lyrically sounded out and given its due, one at a time. This takes place at every moment in Dickinson's poetry that articulates a plausible way of seeing, in which an aspect of the whole multifaceted truth *may* be disclosed. The poet thereby gives voice to perspectival truth in a musical and concise manner that (when successful) should move us, her readers, to *feel* how things appear to be—from every affective standpoint that she adopts.[40]

REFERENCES

Abrams, M. H. *Natural Supernaturalism: Tradition and Revolution in Romantic Literature.* New York: W. W. Norton & Co., 1971.

Benfey, Christopher E. G. *Emily Dickinson and the Problem of Others.* Amherst: University of Massachusetts Press, 1984.

Brantley, Richard. *Experience and Faith: The Late-Romantic Imagination of Emily Dickinson.* New York: Palgrave Macmillan, 2004.

Cameron, Sharon. *Lyric Time: Dickinson and the Limits of Genre.* Baltimore: Johns Hopkins University Press, 1979.

Carlyle, Thomas. *Sartor Resartus.* Edited by Kerry McSweeney and Peter Sabor. New York: Oxford University Press, 1987.

Cavell, Stanley. *In Quest of the Ordinary: Lines of Skepticism and Romanticism.* Chicago: University of Chicago Press, 1988.

Cavell, Stanley. "Thinking of Emerson." In *The Senses of Walden: An Expanded Edition,* 121–138. Chicago: University of Chicago Press, 1992.

Coleridge, Samuel Taylor. *Biographia Literaria.* 2 vols. Edited by John T. Shawcross. Oxford: Clarendon Press, 1907.

Deppman, Jed. *Trying to Think with Emily Dickinson.* Amherst: University of Massachusetts Press, 1998.

Dickinson, Emily. *Letters of Emily Dickinson.* Edited by Mabel Loomis Todd. Cleveland: World Publishing Company, 1951.

---

40. I am indebted to Eileen John for numerous helpful comments, and to Elisabeth Camp for editorial suggestions that helped me to find my focus. For illuminating conversations about Dickinson's poetry, I thank: Richard Eldridge, Paul Friedrich, Oren Izenberg, Maria Alexandra Keller, Victor Kestenbaum, David Mason, Edward F. Mooney, Karin Nisenbaum, J. P. Rosensweig, Ruth Rebecca Tietjen, and Bruce Smith. Alice Xiang provided invaluable research assistance.

Dickinson, Emily. *The Letters of Emily Dickinson*. 3 vols. Edited by Thomas H. Johnson and Theodora Ward. Cambridge, MA: Harvard University Press, 1958.

Diehl, Joanne Feit. *Dickinson and the Romantic Imagination*. Princeton: Princeton University Press, 1981.

Emerson, Ralph Waldo. *Essays and Lectures*. Edited by Joel Porte. New York: Library of America, 1983.

Emerson, Ralph Waldo. *The Essential Writings of Ralph Waldo Emerson*. Edited by Brooks Atkinson. New York: Modern Library, 2000.

Erfani, Farhang. "Dickinson and Sartre on Facing the Brutality of Brute Existence." In *Emily Dickinson and Philosophy*, edited by Jed Deppman et al., 175–187. Cambridge: Cambridge University Press, 2013.

Farr, Judith. *The Passion of Emily Dickinson*. Cambridge, MA: Harvard University Press, 1992.

Furtak, Rick Anthony. "The Value of Being: Thoreau on Appreciating the Beauty of the World." In *Thoreau's Importance for Philosophy*, edited by Rick Anthony Furtak et al., 112–126. New York: Fordham University Press, 2012.

Hadot, Pierre. *What Is Ancient Philosophy?* Translated by Michael Chase. Cambridge, MA: Harvard University Press, 2002.

Juhasz, Suzanne. *The Undiscovered Continent: Emily Dickinson and the Space of the Mind*. Bloomington: Indiana University Press, 1983.

Keats, John. *Complete Poems and Selected Letters*. New York: Modern Library, 2001.

Kierkegaard, Søren. *Concluding Unscientific Postscript*. Translated by Alastair Hannay. Cambridge: Cambridge University Press, 2009.

Kimpel, Ben. *Emily Dickinson as Philosopher*. Lewiston, NY: Edwin Mellen Press, 1981.

Larmore, Charles. *The Romantic Legacy*. New York: Columbia University Press, 1996.

Lee, Maurice S. "Dickinson's Superb Surprise." *Raritan* 28 (2008): 45–67.

Lee, Maurice S. *Uncertain Chances: Science, Skepticism, and Belief in Nineteenth-Century American Literature*. New York: Oxford University Press, 2012.

Lundin, Roger. *Emily Dickinson and the Art of Belief*. Grand Rapids, MI: William B. Eerdmans Publishing Co., 1998.

McIntosh, James. *Nimble Believing: Dickinson and the Unknown*. Ann Arbor: University of Michigan Press, 2000.

Nietzsche, Friedrich. *On the Genealogy of Morals*. Edited by Walter Kaufmann. New York: Vintage Books, 1989.

Reid, James D. *Being Here Is Glorious: On Rilke, Poetry, and Philosophy*. Evanston, IL: Northwestern University Press, 2015.

Rorty, Richard. *Contingency, Irony, and Solidarity*. Cambridge: Cambridge University Press, 1989.

Thoreau, Henry David. *The Journal of Henry D. Thoreau*. 14 vols. Edited by Bradford Torrey and Francis H. Allen. Boston: Houghton Mifflin, 1949.

Thoreau, Henry David. *Walden: An Annotated Edition*. Edited by Walter Harding. Boston: Houghton Mifflin, 1995.

Thoreau, Henry David. *A Week on the Concord and Merrimack Rivers*. Edited by Carl F. Hovde et al. Princeton: Princeton University Press, 1980.

Vendler, Helen. *Dickinson: Selected Poems and Commentaries*. Cambridge, MA: Harvard University Press, 2010.

Vendler, Helen. *Poets Thinking: Pope, Whitman, Dickinson, Yeats*. Cambridge, MA: Harvard University Press, 2004.

Chapter 2

Interiority and Expression
in Dickinson's Lyrics

MAGDALENA OSTAS

The act of observing the shape of her own inner world provides Emily Dickinson with an inexhaustible subject for poetry. Unlike other poets for whom a self-directed gaze is often occasioned or circumstantially forced, Dickinson has a permanent and vivid sense of the import and significance of her own inner experience, as if life and inner life were synonymous. Her poems give articulation and shape to an expansive range of thoughts, feelings, moods, happenings, ideas, and perspectives, and the kind of attention she pays to inner life is as likely to be meditative or reflective as it is to be critical. Dickinson has an out-of-the-ordinary capacity for impersonally concerning herself with herself, and the imagination and perceptiveness with which she records her own self-imaginings are the mark of her poetic imagination.

The argument I pursue in this essay is that Dickinson's poetics of inner life makes us see anew the long-standing philosophical problem of expression—words and the selves they bespeak. Dickinson's poetry invests itself in an understanding of subjectivity that rearranges

The Poetry of Emily Dickinson. Elisabeth Camp, Oxford University Press (2021). © Oxford University Press.
DOI: 10.1093/oso/9780190651190.003.0003

the anchors and horizons we often turn to in thinking about how lives and identities take on shape in expressive forms. For at the same time that poetry for Dickinson is the medium of reflectiveness, it is also the medium that takes her own interiority out of confinement, where it seems in fact to be useless to her. Poetry, strangely, forces this essentially inward poet to conclude that introspection leads to blindness and variations of ignorance rather than to self-knowledge and understanding. As a medium of expressiveness, poetry allows Dickinson to reach herself by giving her evidence of herself—not in general or comprehensively, but in allowing her to encounter the particular *what* and *how* of her own inner life as it takes shape outside of her. Poetry lets Dickinson turn herself inside out, but not so as to disclose the substance of her inner world but so as to be able to perceive and encounter it at all. Dickinson experiments with lyric subjectivity in uncommon ways, and she presents us with a new picture of a human subject unable to find comfort or satisfaction in continuing to pursue itself *in there*. This constitutes a deliberate hypothesis about what we are and how we come to know who we are.

In this creative conception of what it means to write in which words exhibit selves with concreteness and substance, Dickinson proves to be one of the best literary thinkers we have on the topic of self-expression. Her perspective on the concept of expression comes to us as ideas that take on life and course around within the lyric form, a perspective registered in what her readers often have called Dickinson's acts of poetic thinking.[1] Often the poet herself

---

1. The associations readers of Dickinson have made between her lyricism and her "thinking" often have been suggestive. Allen Tate, for example, registers the power of Dickinson's poems not to convey abstractions themselves but to give those abstractions sensuous form and illumination ("Emily Dickinson," 218–221). In a similar train of thought, Helen Vendler asks how Dickinson's attraction to tenseless thinking and the "philosophical stasis" of the mind relates to her "chromatic" and "serial" habits of writing ("Emily Dickinson Thinking," 49–50). And Jed Deppman rightly reminds us that the key to understanding the ideas alive in Dickinson's poems lies in finding the connection between her forms of mental

tells us that she is overwhelmingly occupied with the topic of human identity and its manifestation or incarnation in expressive forms like poems: how "The Outer - from the Inner / Derives it's magnitude - " (Fr 450, J 451; 1862), or how a word in actuality can be "made Flesh" and "breathes distinctly" (Fr 1715, J 1651). What literature and philosophy at their intersection can gain by engaging the idea that poems pursue and probe hypotheses about subjectivity and expression will concern me centrally in this essay.

It is important to register just how forcefully each one of Dickinson's poems challenges the idea that expressive acts make visible, legible, or tangible a hidden and unencounterable realm of experience that stays on the "inside" until we precisely express it. The domain of this inward poet is so rarely confession or self-disclosure. Dickinson dislodges her image of words breathing and becoming flesh entirely from a logic of pressing thoughts or feelings outward from the inside. Instead, Dickinson's verse is almost wholly absorbed by the project of attentively and microscopically recording our attempts and search for expression—the ways we "reckon" (Fr 533, J 569; 1863), "measure" (Fr 550, J 561; 1863), and "discern" (F 620, J435; 1963) who we are and how the things and affairs of the world impact us. These are the poet's courageous, vital, and deliberate attempts to give the inner life coherence and shape. Dickinson abandons the picture of poetry as a mirror for the mind or spirit, but

experimentation and the seeming necessity of recording these experiments in poetic language (*Trying to Think with Emily Dickinson*, 57). In the try-to-think-death poems, Deppman argues for example, the taking on of a particular poetic perspective allows Dickinson to record what he calls "the permanent impotence of thought before death," since choosing to inhabit the space beyond death is a perfectly good thing to do in poem (*Trying to Think*, 204). Deppman might say that, unlike philosophy, poetry lets you *do* that—that is, take on such a perspective—without appearing silly, mad, or just morbid, and that the thought embodied in such a poem is inextricable from the poem's ability compellingly to take on this unique point of view on life at all. The question of why Dickinson pursues the project of thinking in the medium of poetry thus has meaningfully intrigued critics of all kinds.

she also importantly disavows the idea that the same mind or spirit, as if out of desperation, might instead settle for describing the futility or impossibility of reaching for such descriptions. On the contrary, Dickinson takes inspiration from the kinds of understanding we occasion when we "count" (Fr 533) and "wonder" (Fr 550) aloud about ourselves.

Self-understanding, therefore, only surfaces in Dickinson's poems through the creative act itself. In "I would not paint - a picture - " (Fr 348, J 505; 1862), to cite one example, Dickinson asks us to imagine three times how receptiveness is the foundation of the process of artistic creation. She first posits that she would rather be a beholder than a painter, allowed to dwell on and wonder about the picture rather than apply paint. She continues to say in the poem's second stanza, analogously, that she would rather be a listener than a musician, "Raised softly" like a "Balloon" by the music rather than playing an instrument. Then Dickinson's metaphors for receptive and creative activity collide and merge in the poem's final stanza when she imagines herself into the position of poet and reader at once. Being "a Poet" in this final moment entails being able to "stun" not her audience but her own self "With Bolts - of Melody!" Such a capacity simultaneously to be the stunning poet and the one stunned Dickinson calls an "Art," elevating the ability to encounter her own words with the force of astonishment and true surprise to a poetic skill. The image suggests that she hears the words as they make an entry into the world, suddenly concrete, as though they had not issued from her own pen and voice. This conception of writing functions as a strong countercurrent to an understanding of lyric that necessitates a singular, coherent voice that presses its interiority outward. Writing poetry in "I would not paint - a picture - ," contrastingly, has the power to show Dickinson things she otherwise did not know and could not have known and would otherwise not have come to know had she not written *just*

this poem. In this way, poetry for her is revelation and understanding: Poets All (Fr 533).

Since poetry for Dickinson so often appears as a medium of self-
encounter that guides her to new forms of self-understanding, her
lyric experiments frequently demand bending out of shape the first-
person point of view and the integrity of the human body in extraor-
dinary ways. This inclination to split, bisect, haunt, and disunite the
self is familiar to many readers of Dickinson's poetry, and sometimes it registers for Dickinson's readers as indicative of an essential
alienation, a symptom of radical withdrawal, or a mark of the poet's
detachment from her own existence.[2] Yet Dickinson's refusal to give
human subjectivity a basic integrity or oneness is not necessarily the
sign of a self unable to inhabit its own life easefully. For instance, the
distanced point of view that Dickinson's lyrics often manage to con-
struct onto the experiences that their speakers record—the sensations that arise within them, the movements of mind, the contents
of consciousness—is what allows the poems to impress themselves
as forms of perceptive description or lucid observation and not at
all alienated utterance. In moments where she takes palpable delight
in being or becoming "Nobody" (F 260, J288; 1861) to herself,
Dickinson demonstrates how life can be even more compelling of
attention when it appears "So still - so Cool - " (Fr 129, J80; 1859) and
words arrive without being asked, "unsummoned in" (Fr 1243, J 1955;
1872), to capture or describe our experience. In poems like "I felt a
Funeral, in my Brain" (Fr 340, J 280; 1862) or "I felt a Cleaving in my
Mind - " (Fr 867, J 937; 1864), the speaker's self-splitting certainly
betokens mental despair or breakdown, but this is not the only way

---

2. See, for example, Geoffrey Hartman's representative comment that in her self-observations
Dickinson manages to "elide the agony of self-consciousness" because her "slightly apart"
perspective on herself is essentially "spectatorial"—that is, bizarrely unmoved by her own
self-directed gaze ("Language from the Point of View of Literature," 350).

Dickinson splits selfhood. While "The first Day's Night had come - " (Fr 423, J 410; 1862) also takes madness as its theme, for example, the poem also interrogates selfhood from a perspective that discovers discontinuity between a past and a present self from the point of view of feeling such a discontinuity in the present tense. When Dickinson writes in the poem "That person that I was - / And this One - do not feel the same - ," she registers a feeling or *sensation* that is incited by her "giggling" brain, one that bursts the continuity of time and identity. It is as though the poet were recording the outline of a thought experiment intended to spook herself. Similarly, what Dickinson calls "yawning Consciousness" in "I never hear that one is dead" (Fr 1325, J 1323; 1874) confronts the speaker not as a repository of thought but as an encounter with a gaping blankness that the poet needs courage just to "dare" to stage. Dickinson's readiness to break up and sunder selfhood in these ways can be understood as a form of conceptual play from a point of view that comprehends just how uniquely poetry as a medium (unlike traditional philosophical discourse, for instance) allows her to use self-splitting as a form of serious, forceful investigation. Dickinson sees that poetry lets her express her innermost desires and lets her outline the contours of her own mind *only because* it lets her come to lay eyes and ears on them at all, especially since they are not always apparent to her as her very own discrete and recognizable "feelings" or "thoughts."

Dickinson's insight into how we come understand ourselves in expressive acts can be difficult to apprehend within the terms of some of our own contemporary thinking in literature and philosophy about writing and identity. One could argue further that Dickinson's verse actually seems to resist some of the threads of thinking that make up the history of reading her poetry, for the history of reading Dickinson has been dominated by two alternatives for understanding her experiments with writing and inner life: she is either the remarkable transcriber and translator of inner experience, or she is the messenger who reports on the frustrations and final impossibility of such transcriptions. In the most important scholarship that highlights Dickinson's concentration on human interiority, her poetic fixation on the self's inner life casts her in the role of transcriber of the inner world. Dickinson has been understood in this way as a poet who writes in the Romantic tradition of the neurotic soul, as a cultivator of consciousness of religious severity, as a poet whose dedication to inner scrutiny anticipates the psychoanalysts, and as a poet of privacy who harbors a real terror of exposure.[3] Yet anyone who has read Dickinson knows that her self-occupied poetics of the self—strangely—is anything but self-absorbed. Her poems are personal yet wholly impersonal, and the tradition of scholarship that takes Dickinson as the poet of interiority misses the ways her lyrics are feats of formal perspective and impassive attentiveness too.

In an interesting way, the emphasis on Dickinson's fixation on inner life persists in strains of criticism that deny her the status of the poet of inwardness and that trace, instead, how Dickinson's verse registers the impossibility or emptiness of simple self-consciousness. In these lines of criticism, Dickinson still looks within and pays full and constant attention to the inner world, but the self that she finds there is not clearly enclosed, easily transparent, or self-evidently present at all. In other words, this line of reading suggests that Dickinson looks for and does *not* find a picture of her self in the landscape of her own interiority: critics argue that she writes with an alienated distance from her actual body, that her sense of outsidedness marks her own life as "other," that she occupies a position of homelessness and subjective dislocation, and that she is an essential ironist of the human

3. See Wells, *Introduction to Emily Dickinson*; Gelpi, *Emily Dickinson: The Mind of the Poet*; Cody, *After Great Pain: The Inner Life of Emily Dickinson* ; and Benfey, *Emily Dickinson and the Problem of Others*.

subject.[4] What these studies have in common with the contrasting lineage that does take Dickinson to be a poet of interiority is the simple but consequential observation that the inner world occupies the poet unreservedly. They differ only in the philosophical apparatus they employ to understand how the poet's interior explorations are motivated and in what kinds of insights they ultimately culminate.

Some of Dickinson's most insightful contemporary readers can steer us toward avenues of reading outside these alternatives and help us understand more deeply Dickinson's own conceptual investments as they come to unfold in her beautifully contorted experiments with lyric subjectivity. Sharon Cameron, for example, confirms that Dickinson poses the question of the "visibility of interior experience" in inventive ways.[5] Cameron argues that the kind of interior transformations that Dickinson's speakers undergo precipitate an abandoning of unified poetic utterance and that the self's coming to see itself as other is thus a habitual enactment in the poems: "These interior transformations, the ones we are supposed to know and be in control of because they are ours and happen inside us, we frequently fail to know precisely because they are ours and happen inside us. Dickinson, without the aid of her own poems, suffered the same confusion."[6] Cameron underscores here that poetry for Dickinson is the medium in which both feeling and cognition become acquainted with their own shape and their own histories—that is, in which they essentially come to recognize themselves. This is so thoroughly the case that emotions and thoughts appear to make little sense to

4. Hartman, *Criticism in the Wilderness*; Diehl, *Dickinson and the Romantic Imagination*; Crumbley, *Inflections of the Pen: Dash and Voice in Emily Dickinson* ; and Deppman, *Trying to Think with Emily Dickinson.*

5. Cameron, *Lyric Time*, 26.

6. Cameron, *Lyric Time*, 47. For a compelling extension of this argument, see also Cameron, *Choosing Not Choosing*, 186.

Dickinson without the benefit of the tentative coherence that poems can give them.

Like Cameron, Virginia Jackson can help us see how important it is for Dickinson to write and think beyond the familiar alternatives of self-revelation or self-effacement that the broader history of reading her lyrics seems to hold out. Jackson reminds us that Dickinson's poems are not the "temporally self-present" or "unmediated" lyrics of the soul they so frequently are taken to be and that they are anchored essentially to the circumstances of their origination and circulation.[7] Jackson criticizes interpretations of Dickinson's verse that wipe out the contingent details that animate and frame her poems ("referents, genres, enclosures, circumstances, addressees, occasions, secrets"[8]), and she argues that Dickinson's speakers too often collapse into a generic and universal idea of a lyric voice. In the corrective she offers to the notion that Dickinson's lyrics are forms of "a private language addressed—lyrically—to all of us,"[9] Jackson draws attention to the ways Dickinson's lyrics suspend, confuse, or (in all the best cases) creatively reanimate classic questions about the self's relationship to its forms of expressiveness.

Dickinson in these ways thinks *through* her poems, continually using them to interrogate how the self can make or create itself—in effect, arrive at itself. There are striking connections between this unique poetics of the self and several strains in contemporary philosophy, aesthetics, and literary criticism that reconceive the concept of expression in an analogous way. For philosophers and literary theorists often inspired by the later Wittgenstein like Stanley Cavell, Charles Taylor, Richard Eldridge, Garry Hagberg, and Charles Altieri—as for Dickinson—self-knowledge is not merely bound to

7. Jackson, *Dickinson's Misery*, 9.
8. Jackson, *Dickinson's Misery*, 98.
9. Jackson, *Dickinson's Misery*, 165.

creative expression but is rather continuously made up of it.[10] One might say that the defining thread in this contemporary line of thinking about subjectivity is the insight that we elucidate ourselves to ourselves in expressive acts, and we acquire awareness of ourselves only as we become visible in our triumphs and tangles of words. It is as if there isn't that much to us before the moment of making ourselves known, which turns out to count for nearly everything. The self for these philosophers and literary critics is never conceived as an inner space permeated by a set of thoughts, a concrete feeling, or a perceived mood. Here is Charles Taylor on this important point about selfhood: "A human life is seen as manifesting a potential which is also being shaped by this manifestation; it is not just a matter of copying an external model or carrying out an already determinate formulation."[11] Richard Eldridge similarly emphasizes the constructive role of expression in the constitution of the self: "Instead of recording an external reality that is given, speech and other expressive activities release a human identity that is wedded to aspirations that thereby come into articulate existence."[12] And Garry Hagberg gives an insightful account of human expression also grounded in an understanding of expressive activity as a creative form of self-knowledge:

> Knowing oneself is thus not a matter of introspecting, in the metaphysical sense of the term, on the inner object contained in one's private Cartesian interior. It is, rather, a matter of introspection very differently understood, a matter of reflecting on oneself

10. See, for example, Cavell, *Must We Mean What We Say?*, *The Claim of Reason*, and *Philosophy the Day after Tomorrow*; Taylor, "Language and Human Nature" and "Theories of Meaning," and *Sources of the Self*; Eldridge, *The Persistence of Romanticism: Essays in Philosophy and Literature* and *Literature, Life, and Modernity*; Hagberg, *Art as Language*, "Autobiographical Consciousness," and *Describing Ourselves*; and Altieri, "Towards an Expressivist Theory of the Affects," and *Reckoning with the Imagination*.

11. Taylor, *Sources of the Self*, 375.

12. Eldridge, *Persistence of Romanticism*, 56.

and one's actions—one's words, deeds, gestures, thoughts, second thoughts, hopes, fears, aspirations, doubts, wishes, needs, and countless other things that take a central (or perhaps informatively peripheral) place when recalling the actions and utterances and the context within which they took place.[13]

What philosophers like Taylor, Eldridge, and Hagberg find important in their reconstruction of the concept of "expression" is the idea that attempts to grasp the self as an abstraction have to fail because they in effect extricate the self from the actual horizons and cares of its very own life. For these philosophers, you have to see yourself and see what you do and create *out there* before you are willing to say what motivates you, what kind of shape or horizons you have, and who you are.

The parallel idea about selfhood that animates Dickinson's lyrics is that what might be understood as one's "self" or "Being" is not something in one's physical possession or within one's palpable inner sensory range. Dickinson is never clear about who she is, and so she turns toward her own utterances to try to find out. Put simply, this means that for Dickinson the shape of a self cannot be grasped in a single moment, and it also cannot be understood from the inside. The self in this way is not a substance or a thing but a "wherein" of activity. In her poems Dickinson shows again and again that the nature of selfhood demands that we look for, reach toward, glimpse, feel out, and come to see our selves as those selves manifest and contort in various outward expressive forms, each one revealing and shrouding an ever-developing human identity in a different way. We will see this unique dynamic of self-encounter closely as it unfolds in three different poems: "I felt my life with both my hands" (Fr 357, J 351; 1862),

---

13. Hagberg, *Describing Ourselves*, 105.

"One need not be a Chamber - to be Haunted - " (Fr 407, J 670; 1862), and "I heard a Fly buzz - when I died - " (Fr 591, J 465; 1863).

The way poetry seems to let Dickinson apprehend her very being and sketch an outline of herself from the inside can be her explicit topic in a poem. In "I felt my life with both my hands," for example, she imagines forms of self-investigation concretely:

I felt my life with both my hands
To see if it was there -
I held my spirit to the Glass,
To prove it possibler -

I turned my Being round and round
And paused at every pound
To ask the Owner's name -
For doubt, that I should know the sound -

I judged my features - jarred my hair -
I pushed my dimples by, and waited -
If they - twinkled back -
Conviction might, of me -

I told myself, "Take Courage, Friend -
That - was a former time -
But we might learn to like the Heaven,
As well as our Old Home"!

(Fr 357, J 351; 1862)[14]

Here Dickinson makes material the impulse to take oneself as an object of inspection. "Who is this, and what is this body?" her speaker

14. Texts for Dickinson's poems are from *The Poems of Emily Dickinson*, ed. R. W. Franklin (Cambridge, MA: The Belknap Press of Harvard University Press, 1999). References to this edition appear in the text abbreviated as *Fr*, followed by the poem's number.

seems to ask. There are two parts to the speaker figured in the poem, the physical part that is unanimated and seems suddenly strange, and the conscious part that is dynamically wondering about its own life-lessness, eager to probe itself so that it can come to recognize itself again. The temptation for readers of the poem, therefore, has been to understand Dickinson's feeling-her-own-life straightforwardly, that is, as a set-up or scene in which she makes contact with her own body using her senses. Because Dickinson's speaker describes seeking out who or what she is in these stanzas, the poem decidedly does capture an essential sense of disorientation and dislocation. The speaker's confusion can be read as a symptom of some tribulation or even a serious trauma, so that she seems to emerge out of a difficult experience directly into the first line of the poem on the page, reaching out for and trying to feel her own life with her hands, seeking a renewed link to her own experience.

For readers of "I felt my life with both my hands" who exemplify the line of reading in which Dickinson's speaker is allowed to encounter herself, the speaker posthumously examines her own body: she first lays hands on her corpse, then sounds out abstract markers of her identity ("Being," "name"), and finally stirs and prods her own face for familiar signs of vitality.[15] In this interpretive scenario Dickinson's speaker seems to stand hovering above her deceased self. Reading the imagery in the poem like this conjures a sense of mock-Gothic irony that recalls the more overtly ironic poem "One need not be a Chamber - to be Haunted - " (Fr 407, J 670; 1862). In the humorous sustained metaphor that structures that poem, the self's division unfolds as a parody of Gothic tropes that cast the proverbial chilling stranger within one's chamber as a part of oneself, the part capable of disrupting the whole. Robert Weisbuch describes Dickinson's

---

15. Farland, " 'That Tritest/Brightest Truth,' " 382–84.

stranger within usefully as her sense of "internal externality."[16] In "One need not be a Chamber" the poet appears to take pleasure in tracing out the analogy that occurs to her between the mystery of the corridors in a "House" and those in a mind or "Brain," and she reaffirms the parallel when she writes that the "Assassin hid in our Apartment" is actually "Ourself behind ourself, concealed - ." The fact that strangeness turns out to be immanent makes "One need not be a Chamber" in the end a comical poem, because Dickinson's image for a divided self (a too-literal specter in a haunted house) makes it impossible to register her picture of self-haunting with seriousness. The poem thus manages to suspend the difficult implications of its own hypothesis about identity because its caricatured ghost, a fig- ure supposed to symbolize a central part of ourselves or to capture a distressing but real condition of selfhood, in actuality distances the stranger within completely.

"I felt my life with both my hands," in contrast, takes up the impli- cations of Dickinson's vision of selfhood with consequence. The most valuable way to evacuate the poem of the image of a speaker feeling her own lifeless corpse is to remember that in the opening stanzas Dickinson does not in fact purport to feel her body but instead her "life" and "spirit," and then later her "Being." We can certainly retain the sense that the poet makes literal, material contact ("felt") with herself in the poem's opening moment, but there is no reason at all to think that what she feels is unanimated flesh. Further, the hypo- thetical sensation of making contact with one's own no-longer-vital body carries an array of resonances fundamentally different from how we might imagine the sensation of once again coming to feel- one's-life. The latter is actually a heartening feeling that conveys the speaker's sudden *self-understanding* through an image of touching something with one's hands, immediate and palpable. Dickinson's

16. Weisbuch, *Emily Dickinson's Poetry*, 140.

speaker suddenly feels-her-life in the sense that her own experience, at times seeming to her faraway and vague, suddenly becomes vivid and accessible again. The opening image of touching one's life conveys a feeling of brightness and relief and not morbid alienation. That the speaker reaches out to touch her life because she does not know "if it was there" similarly need not mean that she has grown cold and needs to take a pulse on her existence. We might instead understand the images Dickinson builds in the poem, most directly in its second line, as a form of questioning directed not at the *whether* but at the *what* of her life: she reaches out to feel not just *that* her life is there but pursues the deeper question of its physical shape and abstract meaning. As Dickinson reaches out to herself in this poem, she does not ask, "Am I still alive?" but rather "Who in the world am I?"

It turns out in "I felt my life with both my hands" that Dickinson's speaker is not split into an observed- and observing-self at all. On the contrary, the process of the speaker's feeling-her-life slowly begins to empty the poem of its sense of self-division, since what the speaker experiences is a tangible reawakening of the link between the two parts of herself. The gradual arrival of self-recognition and gladness for again coming into contact with her own experience is the central feeling that the poem strives to convey: she *felt her life* with both her hands, she reports in the first line, as if surprised that experience could again yield such a familiar sensation. The subtleties of Dickinson's play with first-person perspective are thus both more simple and more complex than the truisms about self-division in her poetry would suggest. This poem's opening image makes us see not only that the self can feel intensely unfamiliar to itself but also that this sense of being unfamiliar to oneself is a more simple or primary feeling than the paradoxically more difficult ability to "feel-one's-life." The latter for Dickinson seems to be a remarkable and unusual sensation worth dwelling on. Strangely, conveying this surprising sense of oneself as familiar necessitates an image of inhabiting two bodies at the same time, but in the interest of illustrating that the subject is not "split" but precisely comfortable again, however tentatively or momentarily. The speaker in the poem, in other words, stages the transition between feeling strange to herself and once again feeling like an inhabitant of her own life.

What precipitates self-recognition in "I felt my life with both my hands" is a series of images in which the speaker handles the parts of herself that appear to have taken on a life of their own: first touching and handling her life as if it were a tactile object; then deliberately taking up her "Being" in active, circular mental ruminations; and finally speaking and asking aloud after the "Owner's" name, which she confesses she might not recognize as her own if she were to hear it. It makes sense that the parts of the self that Dickinson's speaker finds out in the world at first alarm or surprise her. For ways like this of coming to identify with one's own external expressions press the question of how things made up of materials, sounds, or words can still be said (as Dickinson puts it in the poem) to be "of me" at all. I am not made up of materials, sounds in the air, or words on the page—and yet I am. How does the Soul settle into places other than my body? Dickinson professes, as a poet, an essential wonder and astonishment at the fact that selves can be made up of words and things, and that we can thus at times apprehend ourselves outside ourselves. Dickinson's images capture the state that confronting our own lives and selves from without can precipitate, and they acknowledge that such confrontations with signs and pieces of ourselves laid out in the world can sometimes bring a knowledge so new and unfamiliar that our older self (as in Nietzsche) has to die in order to make room for a fully transformed self-understanding.

Dickinson motivates the impulse to speak in "I felt my life with both my hands" by suggesting that she doesn't feel her life at all in the space before the poem begins, so that the occasion for poetic utterance is explicitly the desire to convey the sudden and surprising ability to feel-one's-life. In the poem the occasion for speaking—diegetically—is no-longer-knowing-oneself and consequently telling us that she then *does* come to feel her life, more and more, over the course of the poem. The comfort and relief that self-recognition brings enter the poem only as she agrees to make explicit the urge to reach out and touch her life with her hands and turn it "round and round" in her head, giving the impulse toward self-investigation a series of beautiful poetic figures that make the longing concrete. This impulse, again, doesn't betoken an empty self but, instead, confirms the speaker's confusion and curiosity about the paths her own development has taken: my life slipped out of my reach, but now I can feel it again, and with my very own hands!

Dickinson's powerful attention to a difficult dimension of selfhood in this poem gets lost in logical, corporeal impossibilities and an inevitable ironic overlay as long as her speaker is thought to confront her own corpse (or, in other poems, really witness the funeral in her own brain, or actually live to convey the truth of a posthumous fly). As Kathleen Anne Peterson reminds us, Dickinson's first-person voice is characterized by far-reaching formal manipulations through which the poet speculates about just how far she should expand the terrain subjectivity is allowed to inhabit.[17] Like the mysterious image of dissipating mist in the air that Virginia Woolf uses throughout *Mrs. Dalloway* as a metaphor for human identity, Dickinson's own cryptic representations of selfhood can be difficult to access because of the conceptual stretches they necessitate and physical impossibilities they insist on. How can a person with a human body be mist-like? How can I touch my life with my own hands? How can you hear something after you die? Dickinson's images for untethered selfhood thus demand a form of "referentless"[18] or

17. Kathleen Anne Peterson, "Supposed Person: Emily Dickinson and the Selflessness of Poetry" (PhD diss., Harvard University, 2006), 24.
18. Porter, *Dickinson*, 123.

"sceneless"[19] reading, one that is indifferent to the contextual conti-
nuities a scene calls for and that is simultaneously deeply interested
in circumstantial human experience.

Like "I felt my life with both my hands," Dickinson's famous poem
about hearing a fly buzz the moment of her own death seems to demand
that we split the speaker up into a body and an attendant mind curious
about that body's experience. Dickinson's speaker seems to straddle life
and death in "I heard a Fly buzz - when I died - ," placing one foot tentatively in the world of the afterlife and keeping the other behind so as to
be able to register the sound of the buzzing earth-anchored fly:

> I heard a Fly buzz - when I died -
> The Stillness in the Room
> Was like the Stillness in the Air -
> Between the Heaves of Storm -
>
> The Eyes around - had wrung them dry -
> And Breaths were gathering firm
> For that last Onset - when the King
> Be witnessed - in the Room -
>
> I willed my Keepsakes - Signed away
> What portion of me be
> Assignable - and then it was
> There interposed a Fly -
>
> With Blue - uncertain - stumbling Buzz -
> Between the light - and me -
> And then the Windows failed - and then
> I could not see to see -

(Fr 591, J 465; 1863)

19. Weisbuch, "Prisming Dickinson; or, Gathering Paradise by Letting Go," 200.

The temptation to understand the scene in this poem as a faithful description of the moment of dying is especially strong because the rules of the human body do not outright exclude the contortions of perspective that the physical context requires. It is possible, in other words, that the buzzing of a fly is the last thing the speaker hears before she dies and that the only puzzle to account for is her desire and posthumous ability to report back and write the poem with the fly's buzzing at its center. It is also possible that when we begin dying, the human sense of hearing clings to the world more adamantly than our other senses, surpassing them all in duration by just a little, and that the ability to hear is thus under some empirical understanding the last sense to go. It is conceivable that Dickinson's speaker is not technically alive as she continues to hear the buzzing of the fly. Perhaps in fixating on sound, Dickinson has described more accurately what it might be like the moment when the body passes away.

But it is also possible that Dickinson wants to remind us in this poem that a part of seeing our own existence is glimpsing that existence from the outside and taking seriously the revelations that such discomfiting and dislocating perspectives can return. In the same way that for Dickinson we cannot hide our selves from the world and stash them away inside our heads or torsos, as though our souls were secrets or tightly wrapped packages, the world similarly cannot hide the realities of living a life from us. All we have to do is explore anyway, defiantly in verse, the terrains that our bodies cannot visit. Letting us imagine and inhabit spaces that we normally do not encounter is the domain of things like poems, novels, daydreams, and conversations with other people. There is no reason to think that such imaginative crossings should expand our sense of who we are and what the world is in ways that are always comfortable or secure. And understanding that we cannot hold on to who we imagine we are, Dickinson shows, can be as terrifying as imagining death.

In "I heard a Fly buzz - when I died - " the figure of the fly usurps a set of competing conjectures about death, and it thus has the force of a "truth" that is fundamentally harsh. But its harshness does not lie in its qualities as a figure, as though flies were severe or otherwise menacing creatures, but instead from its power to replace so instantly a set of deep-rooted expectations and beliefs. Weisbuch, for example, maintains that the fly is a "dramatic disappointment" since the poem also evokes "the King" that we would actually hope to witness on the deathbed.[20] Helen Vendler reads the insect as a deliberately hostile image, a counter-picture to a "winged Psyche-soul rising like a butterfly from the discarded body," and she maintains that Dickinson's uncompromising deflation of ascension approaches blasphemy.[21] Kirkby's reading of the fly as a signal of the decomposition and decay of the physical body suggests that the harsh truth of death comes immediately to the dying, as fast as an insect automatically darting to the site of carrion.[22] In all of these cases, the fly's force stems from its capacity to unsettle the most common hopes about other sounds and other images we might make out while passing to the other side. Dickinson's fly can certainly be read as a polemic that instantaneously defeats the myths she has faithfully been taught.

There are also other ways to understand the image of the fly at the center of Dickinson's famous poem. The fly's irritating buzzing, irreducibly fixed onto and emanating from this world, also reminds Weisbuch that Dickinson's stress when she imagines the moment of death falls on the world we will lose rather than on what we are supposed to gain in another life.[23] The fly's energetic buzzing attracts the speaker's mind and senses without her effort or acquiescence—part annoying disturbance amidst "Stillness" that she cannot shoo away,

20. Weisbuch, *Emily Dickinson's Poetry*, 100–101.
21. Vendler, *Dickinson*, 268.
22. Kirkby, *Emily Dickinson*, 102.
23. Weisbuch, *Emily Dickinson's Poetry*, 101.

part emblem of the ordinary vitality of this world we normally do not notice. It is worth remembering that it is constitutive of Dickinson's imaginary about hearing the sound of the fly that she has already died, so that it is not quite right to say that "she hears" it. Instead, we might say that her body registers the buzzing of the fly, and that her mind becomes aware that her body can hear it and reflects on its impression, as though she weren't exactly the person hearing the sound. This is an important distinction between simple hearing and understanding-that-one-hears, a distinction Cameron underlines when she observes that the fly comes forward in the poem as a figure that the speaker has not yet had the chance (and will not have the chance) to invest with the usual meanings and symbolic weights, so that it does not, strictly speaking, relate to and affect "her" and instead just stumbles and buzzes around her body.[24] Michael Clune brings into focus this fact about the poem's communication of sensory experience when he writes that "the speaker recounts a state in which experience is happening, but that experience's relation to her has been severed," so that there is "no sense of experience as the experience of a particular person" and instead only "the subjectlessness of absorbed listening."[25] What is remarkable about Dickinson's poem from this point of view is her ability to recount first-person experience as if it were not her own first-person experience.

In "I heard a Fly buzz - when I died - " Dickinson is actively curious about what happens to her body without her. That Dickinson would posit and affirm her body's ability to register the world without her supervision or assistance, and that she would find her own pictures of this strange receptive ability so compelling, tells us a lot about the way she imagined the human subject and the world of its interiority. She has no hesitation about abandoning her own insides.

---

24. Cameron, *Lyric Time*, 113.
25. Clune, "How Poems Know What It's Like To Die," 637–639.

As Dickinson tells us later, she was in fact "afraid to own a Body - " and "afraid to own a Soul - ," partly because such "Possession" in this life was not "optional" (*Fr* 1050). Since she was in effect stuck and did not have the option of disowning her Body or her Soul, she set out instead to trace out and understand what she owned. Dickinson quickly found that she could not actually see herself when she looked within, and so she looked more intently than any other poet for herself in places other than in her heart and in her mind. Her lyric "I" set out adventurously for views of her body and soul from without, and she found signs, reflections, and figures of herself in the world as she expanded the terrains her own human perspective was allowed to traverse. The insights these perspectives on her own existence returned made her at once ever less certain about and increasingly in awe of what poems have the ability to reveal.

REFERENCES

Altieri, Charles. "Towards an Expressivist Theory of the Affects." *Soundings: An Interdisciplinary Journal* 86, no. 1–2 (2003): 71–102.

Altieri, Charles. *Reckoning with the Imagination: Wittgenstein and the Aesthetics of Literary Experience.* Ithaca and London: Cornell University Press, 2015.

Benfey, Christopher. *Emily Dickinson and the Problem of Others.* Amherst: University of Massachusetts Press, 1984.

Cameron, Sharon. *Lyric Time: Dickinson and the Limits of Genre.* Baltimore and London: Johns Hopkins University Press, 1979.

Cameron, Sharon. *Choosing Not Choosing: Dickinson's Fascicles.* Chicago: University of Chicago Press, 1992.

Cavell, Stanley. *Must We Mean What We Say? A Book of Essays.* Updated ed. Cambridge: Cambridge University Press, 2002 (1969).

Cavell, Stanley. *The Claim of Reason: Wittgenstein, Skepticism, Morality, and Tragedy.* Oxford: Oxford University Press, 1979.

Cavell, Stanley. *Philosophy the Day after Tomorrow.* Cambridge, MA: The Belknap Press of Harvard University Press, 2005.

Clune, Michael. "How Poems Know What It's Like To Die." *ELH* 83, no. 2 (2016): 633–654.

Cody, John. *After Great Pain: The Inner Life of Emily Dickinson*. Cambridge, MA: The Belknap Press of Harvard University Press, 1971.

Crumbley, Paul. *Inflections of the Pen: Dash and Voice in Emily Dickinson*. Lexington: University Press of Kentucky, 1997.

Deppman, Jed. *Trying to Think with Emily Dickinson*. Amherst and Boston: University of Massachusetts Press, 2008.

Diehl, Joanne. *Dickinson and the Romantic Imagination*. Princeton: Princeton University Press, 1981.

Eldridge, Richard. *The Persistence of Romanticism: Essays in Philosophy and Literature* Cambridge: Cambridge University Press, 2001.

Eldridge, Richard. *Literature, Life, and Modernity*. New York: Columbia University Press, 2008.

Farland, Maria Magdalena. "'That Tritest/Brightest Truth': Emily Dickinson's Anti-Sentimentality." *Nineteenth-Century Literature* 53, no. 3 (1998): 364–389.

Gelpi, Albert. *Emily Dickinson: The Mind of the Poet*. Cambridge, MA: Harvard University Press, 1965.

Hagberg, Garry. *Art as Language: Wittgenstein, Meaning, and Aesthetic Theory*. Ithaca: Cornell University Press, 1995.

Hagberg, Garry. "Autobiographical Consciousness: Wittgenstein, Private Experience, and the 'Inner Picture.'" In *The Literary Wittgenstein*, edited by John Gibson and Wolfgang Huemer, 228–250. London and New York: Routledge, 2004.

Hagberg, Garry. *Describing Ourselves: Wittgenstein and Autobiographical Consciousness*. Oxford: Oxford University Press, 2008.

Hartman, Geoffrey. "The Voice of the Shuttle: Language from the Point of View of Literature." In *Beyond Formalism: Literary Essays 1958–1970*. New Haven: Yale University Press, 1970, 337-55.

Hartman, Geoffrey. *Criticism in the Wilderness: The Study of Literature Today*, 2nd ed. New Haven: Yale University Press, 2007.

Jackson, Virginia. *Dickinson's Misery: A Theory of Lyric Reading*. Princeton: Princeton University Press, 2005.

Peterson, Kathleen Anne. "*Supposed Person: Emily Dickinson and the Selflessness of Poetry.*" PhD diss., Harvard University, 2006.

Porter, David. *Dickinson: The Modern Idiom*. Cambridge, MA: Harvard University Press, 1981.

Tate, Allen. "Emily Dickinson." In *The Man of Letters in the Modern World: Selected Essays 1928–1955*. New York: Meridian Books, 1955, 211–226.

Taylor, Charles. "Language and Human Nature" and "Theories of Meaning." In *Human Agency and Language: Philosophical Papers*. Cambridge: Cambridge University Press, 1985, 214–247 and 248–291.

Taylor, Charles. *Sources of the Self: The Making of the Modern Identity*. Cambridge, MA: Harvard University Press, 1989.

Vendler, Helen. *Dickinson: Selected Poems and Commentaries*. Cambridge, MA, and London: Belknap Press of Harvard University Press, 2010.

Vendler, Helen. "Emily Dickinson Thinking." *Parnassus: Poetry in Review* 26, no. 1 (2001): 34–56.

Weisbuch, Robert. *Emily Dickinson's Poetry*. Chicago: University of Chicago Press, 1972.

Weisbuch, Robert. "Prisming Dickinson; or, Gathering Paradise by Letting Go." In *The Emily Dickinson Handbook*, edited by Gudrun Grabher, Roland Hagenbüchle, and Cristanne Miller, 197–223. Amherst: University of Massachusetts Press, 1998.

Wells, Henry. *Introduction to Emily Dickinson*. New York: Hendricks House, 1959.

Chapter 3

How to Know Everything

OREN IZENBERG

I could die - to know -
'Tis a trifling knowledge -
News-Boys salute the Door -
Carts - joggle by -
Morning's bold face - stares in the window -
Were but mine - the Charter of the least Fly -

(Fr 537, J 570; 1863)

I.

This is an odd and intense moment for caring about literature. The daily unfolding of history that beggars the imagination can make the work of the imagination in pursuit of new forms or new themes seem trifling, like the expenditure of intellectual energies, material resources, and institutional will that might be better devoted elsewhere. Or, on the other hand, it might seem crucially necessary, like the sort of thing one could die for. Art has historically been a means of last resort; a way, when all other ways are blocked, to envision futures and conceive of alternative lives, or alternative relations to life. The pressure of the present gives rise in our present—as it does in every present—to both reductionist and maximalist accounts of art.

The Poetry of Emily Dickinson. Elisabeth Camp, Oxford University Press (2021). © Oxford University Press.
DOI: 10.1093/oso/9780190651190.003.0004

On the reductionist side: The overwhelming tendency in the literary criticism of the present is to offer historicist answers to any question of literary value. By historicist, I mean to indicate not only the methodological premise that our accounting of a work's value has changed and will change with the times, but also the premise that our interest in the art object is itself of interest insofar as it is diagnostic of *other* sorts of interest: libidinal, economic, political; each also bound to its time. Art objects become occasions for opening windows onto the field of cultural production, and, perhaps, with sufficient industry and ingenuity, onto the field of *general* production in which the art-world is embedded.

Our accounts of what an artwork can do or show are entailments of what we think it *is*: of what it is made, and what powers have generated it. And so these accounts—broadly historical or narrowly sociological—are most often (though not, I think, necessarily) partnered with arguments for an institutional ontology of art; and thus tend toward a sort of skepticism or nominalism about poetry.[1] To call something a poem, on this account, is a kind of honorific: a way of naming some large ambitions for language. And as good as reductionist theories are at giving accounts of the particular shape of these ambitions and explaining why people care or have cared about them, they are at the very least agnostic about the question of whether we *should* care about poems. At their extremes, they aim to rebuke the potential carer-about-art with intimations of the transient and suspect nature of his or her own motives and values.

On the maximalist side, there are, perhaps overwhelmingly in our discipline at present, answers in the key of Adorno, which read in the completeness and ardency of a poem's apparent autonomy from the

---

1. For a variety of positions on the institutional argument, see Robert J. Yanal, ed., *Institutions of Art: Reconsiderations of George Dickie's Philosophy* (University Park: Pennsylvania State University Press, 1994).

historical pressures that hem it in on all sides a negative impression left by the crushing weight of social relations. Art refuses. It withholds acknowledgment. It does not countenance the world as it is. This account, too, has its own ontology of the artwork. It couples an account of the interest that Adorno called *commitment* with an account of the form of the artwork, as not so much autonomous from society but as *resistant to it*: "[i]t is not the office of art to spotlight alternatives, but to resist by its form alone the course of the world, which permanently puts a pistol to men's heads."[2]

In the face of both of these accounts of poetry—the reductionist and the maximalist—I will begin by announcing a value-laden premise; and if you won't ride it with me at least speculatively, I won't get very far. The justifications for poetry that seem most desirable to me involve the claim that poems have an epistemic payoff. That is, if poetry isn't interested in helping me to *know* something new about the world *as it is*, I can't claim to be *that* interested in it.

I could stop here to open this proposition up for contestation, in which any number of things would be open to debate. Perhaps there are psychological concerns about my insistence on the value of knowledge: do I have so much pleasure in my life that I can afford to do without more? Or, one might well be concerned with the specific sense in which I am using the *word* "knowledge." After all, even Adorno regarded the negations of form as yielding a cognitive success, albeit of an obscure kind: All aesthetic questions, he wrote in the "Draft Introduction" to *Aesthetic Theory*, "terminate in those of the truth content of artworks: Is the spirit that a work objectively bears in its specific form true?"[3]

I confess that I don't completely understand what "spirit" means in Adorno's declaration here, and so I don't fully understand how it

2. Adorno, "Commitment," 78.
3. Adorno, Adorno, and Tiedeman, *Aesthetic Theory*, 335.

could be carried "objectively" in a work's "specific form." But granting *something* carried by art's form that was sufficiently truth-like to merit the name, one might wonder whether *epistemology* is the appropriate philosophical base to receive its weight. Here our main interlocutors might be not historicist or sociological, but affect-theoretical: and their objections would be bound up with questions about the *noncognitive* deliverances of poems. There is an open question, for example, about whether the impacts of art, and our embodied responses to them, ought properly to be called knowledge.[4]

But before any such refinements of the debate could be fruitful, it would seem as though I'm obligated to suggest how I can—or if I can—make the object of my preference seem even remotely plausible, so that I even have a side to hold down. It falls to me say how we could, even notionally, come to know things by means of art. The imagination, whatever else we might wish to say about its virtues, does not seem particularly promising as a way of coming to know *facts* about the world. Nor is the justificatory reasoning we encounter in poetry—from premise to conclusion—obviously perspicuous:

> LET man's soul be a sphere, and then, in this,
> Th' intelligence that moves, devotion is;
> And as the other spheres, by being grown
> Subject to foreign motion, lose their own,
> And being by others hurried every day,
> Scarce in a year their natural form obey;
> Pleasure or business, so, our souls admit
> For their first mover, and are whirl'd by it.

---

4. See Pettit, "The Possibility of Aesthetic Realism," : "The affective theorist . . . will say that one is fully entitled to assent to an aesthetic characterization only where one has had a certain noncognitive experience in response to the work and that this naturally leads us to deny that that there can be a non-perceptual title to full 'knowledge' of what the characterization expresses" (25).

Hence is't, that I am carried towards the west,
This day, when my soul's form bends to the East.[5]

Even when a poem like Donne's "Good Friday, Riding Westward"
cultivates the discourse of the logician—with its positing "Let," its
analogical "so," and its conclusory "hence"—one can be persuaded by
the wit of the cosmological argument without finding the argument
persuasive as such. One might say that this is the rhetoric of reason,
rather than the thing itself.

Plato suspected as much, which is why he regarded poetry as at
once parasitic on other forms of knowledge production AND also
divine (by which he meant that whatever wisdom it delivered could
be verified by no reliably replicable principle, but by irrational inspiration alone). Bacon agreed, which is why, when he sought to discover
the place of "poesy" in his *Advancement of Learning*, he ultimately
concluded that while imagination could be an object of science, the
faculty of imagination had no branch of learning to advance, no science appropriate to its own activity: "For as for Poesy, it is rather a
pleasure or play of imagination, than a work or duty thereof."[6]

If poems are in some sense investigatory or even experimental,
their investigations would seem to consist chiefly in demonstrating
what persons can say and their experiments to consist in exemplify-
ing *what words can do.* These are explorations that—whatever their
virtues—don't seem "cognitive" in quite the right way.

What is the right way? We might consider a speculative account
of poetry as a species of thought experimentation: one that could
do more than merely dislodge our entrenched styles of art-making
or conventional habits of thought (these are the things we take

5. John Donne, *Poems of John Donne,* ed. E. K. Chambers, vol. 1. London: Lawrence & Bullen,
1896. 172–173.
6. Bacon, *The Advancement of Learning,* 82.

"experimental writing," typically, to do) but which might actually *produce* knowledge in the way that we hope other kinds of experiments do. Making this case might entail a foray into recent philosophical literature on so-called *conceivability arguments*—the notion that our sheer ability to conceive of some state of affairs has a relation to the claim that that state of affairs is, if not actual, at least possible. As Hume puts it, "nothing of which we can form a clear and distinct idea is absurd and impossible."[7] On this account, *imagination*—understood as our capacity for conceiving of, inventing, depicting, extending ideas—provides access to *modal space*; the space of metaphysical possibility. And with a modal imagination, the conceivability of a thing might be a guide or a goad to the recognition of its possibility. Indeed, the strongest forms of the Humean argument suggest that the link between conceivability and possibility is more than merely suggestion; it is that the conceivability of a thought actually *entails* possibility of a fact.[8]

Arguments for, or from, the modal imagination are powerful; or they would be, if we were convinced by them. But even if we were fully convinced, they have their limits, particularly for art. First, because they are demanding. They require of our dreams that they be unusually thoroughly dreamed: extensive enough to accommodate our propositions, and comprehensive enough to examine for contradiction. Miltonic epic, for example, is centrally concerned with the imaginative justification of metaphysical claims. If I were determined to settle the question of whether the concept of divinity could be reconciled with the doctrine of free action, I might try to imagine a world that validated the following proposition:

---

7. Hume, *David Hume: A Treatise of Human Nature*, 18.
8. For just such a strong account, see Chalmers, "Does Conceivability Entail Possibility?", 145–200.

I formed them free, and free they must remain,
Until they enthrall themselves: I else must change
Their nature, and revoke the high decree
Unchangeable, eternal, which ordained
Their freedom; they themselves ordained their fall.[9]

The attempt to square this particular circle—an unchangeable decree of freedom—might, it turns out, involve imagining a form of monism in which matter and spirit are intertwined—in which, as William Empson imagined, the Godhead must eventually abdicate into Spinozist immanence.[10] Such thoroughly imagined worlds are rare in poetry.[11]

A second limit that the conceivability/possibility link places upon art is that if the link could be true at all, it would be true only in the somewhat constrained sense that what you have learned by submitting the products of the imagination to the discipline of reason is that your conception is metaphysically possible *in some possible world*—though not necessarily in the one we, or anyone, will ever inhabit. This might be adequate for some purposes. A version of the monism I just attributed to Milton might be adequate for the philosopher seeking evidence against reductively materialist or eliminativist accounts of consciousness. But Milton wanted more than that. He wanted to demonstrate that God was inevitable—to *justify*

---

9. *Paradise Lost, The Complete Poetry and Essential Prose of John Milton*, ed. William Kerrigan, 3.124–128, 364.

10. Empson, *Milton's God*.

11. For an interesting argument that entertains the premise that Milton's epic produces knowledge through imaginative projection, but which reaches precisely the opposite conclusion about the substance of that knowledge, see Knapp, *Literary Interest: The Limits of Anti-Formalism*: "Milton intended to project a world in which Christian theism, as he understood it, was true; in fact, however, the world he actually succeeded in projecting was a world in which essential features of his theism revealed themselves to be false" (8).

the ways of god to man—and would have been profoundly unsatisfied to have demonstrated merely that God was not metaphysically incoherent.

So in pursuit of knowledge by imaginative means, I have abandoned the vast majority of poems. Because constructed worlds are demanding, I have abandoned the bulk of poems which do not meet those demands—short poems, non- or skimpily narrative poems; poems less obviously committed to worldbuilding—in favor of the relatively restricted class of epics, hardly any of which exist. I have also, as it were, abandoned myself—marooned myself in the far other seas of merely possible worlds, rather than bringing us closer to the one I reside in.

Wouldn't it be better if the poems we have could help us to know not just something about some world, but anything about our world? Not just about what was possible but about what is the case?

I have already declared that I think it would be *better*; but it still remains to determine how it is *possible*. And so, to compound the barely conceivable with the highly implausible, I want to consider some actually existing poems—chiefly those by Emily Dickinson—alongside some further arguments on behalf of the world's knowability—chiefly those recently offered by the philosopher David Chalmers in his 2012 *Constructing the World*.

II.

Chalmers's ambitious argument resurrects one of the fondest dreams of epistemology: the Laplacean notion that, given a compact set or class of basic truths, a sufficiently powerful intellect in possession of them could range confidently through the realm of knowledge. A being in possession of all the basic truths and capable of perfect reason, Laplace declared, would be in a position to reach to all the rest: "for such an intellect nothing would be uncertain and the future, just like the past would be present before its eyes."[12]

Chalmers calls this thesis about the world "a *scrutability* thesis. It says that the world is in a certain sense comprehensible ... [and] that all truths about the world are *scrutable* from some basic truths" (xiii). For all but the most hard-line skeptic about knowledge, some version of a scrutability thesis is plausible given a generous enough account of the fundamental facts and a humble enough account of the available truths. For Laplace, the relevant truths were physical. For Carnap, who inherits, revises, and extends the idea, they were logical truths. But both of these propositions created some obvious problems for which their authors have been justly taken to task. Some facts do not seem obviously physical or plausibly logical; they are perspectival and subjective, facts about how the world strikes me at a particular moment, or that involve the qualitative features of first-person experiences generally. Some truths depend on how the world is relative to me at a particular moment, marooned as I am at a particular place and time. Elizabeth Barrett Browning described poets as "loyal to the low, and cognizant/ Of the less scrutable majesties"[13]; proposing a version of a scrutability thesis, she reminds us that there are historical, ideological, and social and moral facts to contend with.

Rather than abandon the possibility of scrutability in the face of such hard cases, Chalmers seeks to expand the base just slightly, as little as possible, while still keeping it small enough to make the claim to scrutability nontrivial. A trivial version isn't hard to come by: throw *everything* into the class of "basic facts" and reasoning to anything would be easy. Encode the whole world as a single flaming word, like Jorge Louis Borges's Aleph ("the place where, without admixture or

---

12. Chalmers, *Constructing the World*, xiv.
13. Browning, *Aurora Leigh* (London: J. Miller, 1864). Reprinted: Chicago: Academy Chicago Printers (Cassandra Editions), 1979, 147.

confusion, all the places of the world, seen from every angle, coexist")[14] and you eliminate the need to reason to knowledge at all.[15]

Chalmers's revised and expanded base is not quite so expansive. It includes four classes of facts:

P: "The class of physical truths, including microphysical truths . . . and macrophysical truths":[16] These are truths about what exists and where; the physical truths one can see, as well as those beneath apparent surfaces, and the laws that govern and connect them.

Q: "The class of phenomenal (or experiential) truths."[17] They concern what it's *like* to be in one or another conscious state, whether of sensation, belief, or emotion; together with any psychophysical laws that connect mental states with physical states of matter.

I: A class of "indexical truths,"[18] most prominently including the truths which specify where one is and which time is now. Without access to these facts, we would find ourselves incapable of assessing knowledge claims made relative to place and time: the notion that *today* is Wednesday, or that my name is Emily Dickinson.

T—"A single totality sentence,"[19] is a class containing a single fact, affirming that P, Q, and I are exhaustive; that there are no

---

14. Jorge Luis Borges, "The Aleph," in *Collected Fictions*, trans. Andrew Hurley (New York: Penguin, 1999), 281.
15. Chalmers puts it thus: "We might say that a compact class of truths is a set of truths that involves only a limited class of concepts and that avoids trivializing mechanisms such as coding the entire state of the world into a single number" (xiv).
16. Chalmers, *Constructing the World*, 110.
17. Chalmers, *Constructing the World*, 110.
18. Chalmers, *Constructing the World*, 111.
19. Chalmers, *Constructing the World*, 111.

facts in excess of the world at hand that would render a conclusion drawn on the basis of them incorrect.

From this newly expanded scrutability base, Chalmers argues, it is relatively non-controversial to imagine a Laplacean demon, or a Miltonic angel deriving all knowledge. But what do such figures as oracles have to do with us, who are neither angels nor demons? To address the facts that we are slaves to limit, Chalmers offers us a further thought experiment: an imaginary tool he calls the Cosmoscope.

Imagine in place of your own transformation into the bearer of all relevant basic facts, your possession of an **instrument** that could give you knowledge of the disposition of all objects and persons in the universe. It has the ability to move through space and time to focus on any chosen sector, and show you everything that was physically present within it from the macroscopic to the microscopic. It is capable of prodigious feats of information storage, retrieval, and calculation.

More than a repository of information and calculation about the physical world, the Cosmoscope is a virtual reality device; it can show you what it is like to be any entity at any time *from the inside*: its perceptual, intentional, affective state. Crucially, this need not take place in language. The Cosmoscope can produce, or induce, *direct* knowledge of the phenomenal experience of beings, no matter how like or unlike ourselves they turn out to be. Such knowledge might be had in the form of imaginative states.[20]

This miraculous instrument also conveys indexical truths. Chiefly, it provides its user with the knowledge that you are HERE, NOW; knowledge which would allow its possessor to make inferences from his or her particular state of the physical and experiential world.

20. Chalmers, *Constructing the World*, 116.

Finally, the Cosmoscope can indicate for you one other aspect of the fundamental truths: that they are total, that the world is no bigger than it needs to be to accommodate the truth of P, Q, and I. "T": "T says in effect 'that's all' ":[21] there are no mysteries—or at least none that would invalidate the conclusions you draw based on everything else that you have and are.

Chalmers is under no illusions that a Cosmoscope is in the offing. It is, as he puts it, "a highly fanciful device." Its purpose in his argument is simply to make vivid what an idealized reasoner who entertained the hypothesis of the unity of PQI would be able to do. "The Cosmoscope simply offloads some of the work from ourselves onto the world. In effect, the Cosmoscope takes the burden of storage and much of the burden of calculation. With the aid of a Cosmoscope AND ideal reason, one could come to know anything that could be known." But, Chalmers suggests, "These tools, along with tools for selection and simulation, mean even a non-ideal reasoner can get a long way with a Cosmoscope."[22]

One might imagine that the Cosmoscope presents us with greater problems than mere non-existence: a tool so powerful might well alter the world it purports merely to deliver. And so, to decrease the possibility that our *means* of knowing itself makes full knowledge impossible, Chalmers consents to make the Cosmoscope, already so notional, even more withdrawn:

> We can think of the Cosmoscope as a nonphysical device that interacts with the physical and phenomenal world at only one spatiotemporal location. We can suppose that an individual is locked in a room, that the Cosmoscope ensures that everything outside that room goes on as it would have if the Cosmoscope had

---

21. Chalmers, *Constructing the World*, 111.
22. Chalmers, *Constructing the World*, 117.

not been used, and that the Cosmoscope afterwards removes all traces of it use. . . . We can even minimize the physical impact of a Cosmoscope by supposing that it is a *mental* Cosmoscope: one that conveys information by directly producing certain imaginative states in the subject, and that receives information by monitoring the subject's mental states.[23]

We could even suppose that room is in faraway Amherst, and that the records of these mental operations could be locked away in a camphorwood chest, where the difference they make might be minimized until the world was ready to receive them.

Such passages as these, one might say, don't go any distance toward *justifying* Chalmers's arguments; that is the work of *Constructing the World*, which seeks to draw out the implications of scrutability theses in any number of philosophical domains—epistemology, metaphysics, philosophy of mind, and language. But with these descriptions on the table, one can see, I hope, where I've been headed all along. I would like to entertain the hypothesis that some nontrivial amount of the poetry we actually have tends toward the condition of the Cosmoscope—which means, if nothing else, *that it is invested in the work of knowing in a world that can be known.*

Here are some things that thinking this might entail: First, that some—or perhaps many—poems may coherently be regarded as investigatory devices rather than as primarily aesthetic or rhetorical performances: or, more precisely—that their aesthetic and rhetorical performances should be regarded as a crucial part of their investigatory means. We don't need to invent new kinds of knowing specific to poems.

It might also mean that one is justified in taking an interest in poems on the grounds that they promise to aid their readers in assessing the

23. Chalmers, *Constructing the World*, 135.

character of the world in order to arrive at true conclusions. And it might be correct to evaluate them, at least in part, on whether they succeed.

III.

At this point, arguing for this hypothesis will involve two things: First, it involves a "directed noticing" of certain features of actually existing poems. Second, it involves a willingness to credit poets, at least provisionally, with knowing their own intentions in and for art.

With respect to P, we may note, for example, the profligate mobility and crystalline focus of poems; the way they move us through space to any distant land or nearby spot, from the top of mountains— Mont Blanc or the Himmaleh—to the cruel bottom of the sea; or from the space beyond Earth's atmosphere to the interior of a cell. We note the way poems can encompass great swaths of time, as Auden's "In Praise of Limestone," reveals the geological time of natural processes within "this region / Of short distances and definite places"[24]; or, as in Jorie Graham's "Self Portrait as the Gesture Between Them [Adam and Eve]," the way a poem dilates a moment between two heartbeats until we can examine everything that is inside it.

Emily Dickinson most often traffics in the latter of these: in the subdivision of moments, whether morcellating a traditional poetic unit of the solar day:

> I'll tell you how the Sun rose -
> A Ribbon at a time.

(Fr 204, J 318; 1861)

---

24. W.H. Auden, "In Praise of Limestone," *Collected Shorter Poems 1927–1957* (1948; New York: Random House, 1964), 238–239.

Or else, as in this poem, which breaks time itself into still narrower "ribbons":

> At Half-past Three a single Bird
> Unto a silent Sky
> Propounded but a single term
> Of cautious melody -
>
> At Half past Four, experiment
> Had subjugated test,
> And lo, her silver Principle
> Supplanted all the rest -
>
> At Half-past Seven, element
> Nor implement - be seen -
> And Place, was where the Presence was
> Circumference between -

(Fr 1099, J 1084; 1865)

We can see how, by extending its attentions over the course of four hours like a time-lapse camera, and by subdividing the units of its attention into conspicuously non-symbolic units—the halves, rather than the firm stations of the hours—the poem admits into itself the gradualness of its objects of attention. The knowledge envisioned here is anti-epiphanic; it unfolds like the slow extension of single notes into a melody. And we note also the way that the poem, in providing us first with the elemental units of perception, allows space for the drawing of inferences from data. So that even if, as in this poem, it is difficult for us to say *what* proposition is being reached or affirmed, we may still observe the imagistic translation of the note of birdsong into a "term" of logic; the modulation of first, "cautious" beginnings into a decisive "experiment"; the elevation of a foray in expressive "melody" into a cognitive "Principle." All these transformations support the idea that what initially seems a merely empirical (sonic and temporal) *instance* can support a rational *inference*; and indeed, that at least for a duration, the knowledge of principle that emerges from an unfolding experience "supplants" and makes secondary the particular means by which one has acquired it.

The obscurity of the poem—and it is nothing if not obscure—derives from the nature of the particular object of its knowledge: not what birdsong *is*, but what it was like to hear it. Its knowledge is phenomenal knowledge; by its nature subjective, present only to its possessor, and evanescent, requiring the constant re-affirmation of its presence. (These are, of course, claims about Q which I'll be getting to in a moment.)

Thinking about poetry as knowledge-directed may be counterintuitive in the present. But it does affirm certain kinds of traditional and intuitive stances of the poet toward poems. Knowledge claims underwrite the art, its affective urgency as well as its claims to authority. When we read, for example:

> Ashes denote that Fire was -
> Revere the Grayest Pile
> For the Departed Creature's sake
> That hovered there awhile -
>
> Fire exists the first in light
> And then consolidates
> Only the Chemist can disclose
> Into what Carbonates -

(Fr 1097, J 1063; 1865)

We find a poem that, like "At Half past Three a single Bird," presents us with what I want to call a knowing *attitude*. It records an inference, or a series of inferences. The prior presence of fire is inferred from the denotations of ash; the byproducts, or consolidates of combustion are projected from the presence of flame. These inferences are made on the basis of observed facts; and the poem seems to know a thing or two about processes and laws.

The fact that the poem's vocabulary is scientific may lend a certain privileged sheen to that attitude of knowing; many have noted Dickinson's early interest in and aptitude for the sciences in her brief period of formal education at Amherst Academy and Mt. Holyoke Seminary. But we needn't make too much of this. Her poetry leaves a fair amount to expertise—the Chemist here joins Dickinson's parade of experts: Savans, Philosophers, Geologists who provide her, as it were, secondhand, with facts and laws. I concede that poems—and maybe not even this one—don't seem particularly rich repositories of physical fact or physical law.

My point here is that even if we acknowledge one important way in which poems seem not to resemble the most powerful of Cosmoscopes—they are not supercomputers, capable of tracking the movement of particles; they airily outsource some instances of knowledge to the expert Chemists—it is nonetheless sufficient for my purposes to note that poems are not, by and large, fictions. In them we are not encountering the fictive speech acts of an imagined persona, but language oriented toward the world we inhabit, and aiming at saying something true about it.[25]

It is even more obviously possible (though not wholly uncontroversial) to observe that poems such as we have are invested in the presentation of what Chalmers calls Q: in the vivid provision of interior

---

25. Some poems do unquestionably traffic in entities that can only notionally be said to exist. But not even the most flagrant counterfactuals **necessarily** disqualify a poem from being interested in knowing. Chalmers's remarks on what he calls "the conditional mode" are helpful here:

There are two ways that one can use a Cosmoscope. One can use it in *empirical mode*, as a guide to the world one is in when using the Cosmoscope. In this mode

and subjective states, with a particularity and experiential precision that exceeds our relatively meager repertoire of names for them.

A poem like "Pain - has an Element of Blank - " suggests some of the problems involved in "presenting" the information to be found in Q:

> Pain - has an Element of Blank -
> It cannot recollect
> When it begun - Or if there were
> A time when it was not -
>
> It has no Future - but itself -
> It's Infinite contain
> It's Past - enlightened to perceive
> New Periods - Of Pain.

(Fr 760, J 650; 1863)

What seems to begin as a good faith effort at mental description: one mind seeking to communicate the constituent features or elements of sensation to another in third person terms—"Pain has an element of"—is apparently thwarted by the lack of available sensation terms: by the "Blank" where an explanation should be. And yet the poem goes on to propose a kind of cognitive solution. If the person in pain can neither recall a past different from her present nor conceive of a future in which she will not be in pain, then the lack of

---

the Cosmoscope will tell one about the character of one's own world. One can also use it in *conditional* mode, as a guide to a scenario that may or may not correspond to the world one is in when using the Cosmoscope. In this mode, the Cosmoscope will enable you to reason about how things are *if* that scenario obtains. (117)

A *poetic* Cosmoscope can also work in conditional mode, allowing us to consider what might follow from the presence in the world of ghosts or demons. Perhaps this suggests a way of categorizing poems in relation to how much of the given world they leave intact, or in relation to whether they are making empirical or conditional knowledge claims.

communicative terms does not present a barrier. To conceive the state of pain as lacking alternatives—even for oneself—is to conceive of it as practically universal. Pain is transformed from a mystery— that which must be explained—into a perception, or what Dickenson calls an "enlightenment": something that is vividly possessed and which therefore needs no explanation.

"I felt a Funeral, in my Brain" arrives at a similar conclusion by an alternate route:

> I felt a Funeral, in my Brain,
> And Mourners to and fro
> Kept treading - treading - till it seemed
> That Sense was breaking through -
>
> And when they all were seated,
> A Service, like a Drum -
> Kept beating - beating - till I thought
> My mind was going numb -
>
> And then I heard them lift a Box
> And creak across my Soul
> With those same Boots of Lead, again,
> Then Space - began to toll,
>
> As all the Heavens were a Bell,
> And Being, but an Ear,
> And I, and Silence, some strange Race,
> Wrecked, solitary, here -
>
> And then a Plank in Reason, broke,
> And I dropped down, and down -
> And hit a World, at every plunge,
> And Finished knowing - then -

(Fr 340, J 280; 1862)

It is true that the experience the poem even notionally seeks to present here is not straightforwardly obvious. Helen Vendler, a critic, who, whatever her many virtues, is deeply invested in the normalization of poetry, once declared it to be a poem about what it feels like to fall asleep. Michael Clune understands it as a poem about what it feels like to die.[26] But I would suggest that both of these accounts are themselves attempts to pin a *name* on a blank, on a sensation that has no name. The hallucinogenic quality of the imagery here begins in the realm of metaphor; whatever "it" is, it *feels* like a funeral, albeit one taking place in my brain. And yet as the metaphor extends to take in the ritual rhythms of the service and the treading boots of the pallbearer, it comes to seem less and less metaphorical; less, that is, like a way of pairing an obscure experience with the concept that illuminates it, and more like a way of indicating the pure idiosyncracy and uncommunicability of experience that leaves us marooned within it. In a certain sense, all experiences are experiences of death or sleep. We cannot bring that which is not knowledge into the realm of knowledge without losing its noncognitive phenomenal character.

The singularity of sensations and inner attitudes may be one motive to Dickinson's poem and of its search for an adequate language of description or explanation. But perhaps (as our poet would have it) there is no such language. In this poem we may note Dickinson's recourse not to the figure she draws, but to the treading, beating, and tolling of her verbal performance. Such sounds neither produce nor attest to enclosure in experience; rather, they provide a way of taking experience to be an index to its causes, and so indicate the contours

---

26. Michael W. Clune, "How Poems Know What It's Like to Die," *ELH* 83, no. 2 (2016): 633–654.

of a world whose properties are unconceptualized or unnamed *except* by our experience of them.[27]

Another way of saying this: this poetry takes experience to be idiosyncratic but not private. It conveys experience not discursively, but by exemplification. Poems *induce* imaginative states as the Cosmoscope induces knowledge; and in responding to poetry, we take our own experiences as real knowledge about the world. This may confound our ordinary sense of what it means to know; and thus the ending of the poem doubles down on the idea of ending the *possibility* of knowing. To be "finished knowing" might mean having knowledge finished off, no longer possible. Or it might mean that the work of knowing has achieved completion—finished because one has it all. It might *feel* like the former—like knowledge had evaded your grasp—if you wished to *say* what you knew. But it feels like the latter—like knowledge in hand—if what you wanted was the conviction that you had known something.

I, the Indexical, is the domain of the first person lyric, with its investment in keeping us informed about our location in space, primarily by pointing:

This is a Blossom of the Brain -
A small - italic Seed

(Fr 1112, J 945; 1865)

Indexicality also keeps us located in time, by riding the present of utterance and locating the poem in relation to a constantly unfolding "now":

To-day or this noon
She dwelt so close

---

27. I explore this idea more fully in "Poems Out of Our Heads," *PMLA* 123, no. 1 (2008): 216–222: "Such poetry treats the world as wider and richer (finer grained) than our language for it and so in a certain sense unknown—but not as unknowable" (222).

I almost touched her
Tonight she lies
Past neighborhood
And bough and steeple
Now past surmise

(Fr 1706, J 1702)

Indexicality is, for Chalmers, perhaps the easiest element of the Cosmoscope to imagine: it grounds inferences about past and future by providing its user with the continual knowledge of where she is. But the indexicality of poetry is more complex; as Roland Greene long ago argued, and as Jonathan Culler has recently reaffirmed, poems indicate both a fictive present recorded in the poem as "now," and the real present that we encounter in utterance time.[28] There is no doubt more to say about the complex interplay between utterance time and fictive time; but for the present purpose I simply want to note that these two elements, Q and I, subjectivity and particularity, are the ones most often seen as illicit or disqualifying when it comes to knowledge claims for poetry. In contrast, they are absolutely central for the operation of the Cosmoscope, and to grounding its claims to knowledge.

Finally, poems seem to be notably invested in expressions of T—the totality claim. Poems frequently position themselves at the end of all possible experience in order to provide a solid base for their conclusions: T.S. Eliot presents us in "The Waste Land" with figures of cognitive completion in the person of Tiresias, who has had all empirical experiences, and the Sybil of Cumae, who has seen the future. John Ashbery writes in "As One Put Drunk Into

---

28. Roland Arthur Greene, *Post-Petrarchism: Origins and Innovations of the Western Lyric Sequence* (Princeton, New Jersey: Princeton University Press, 1991). Jonathan Culler, *Theory of Lyric* (Cambridge, MA: Harvard University Press, 2017).

the Packet Boat"—"I tried each thing / only some were immortal and free."[29]

For Dickinson, figures of totality are endemic to the poems. Their most frequent temporal indicator is noon: an hour of undivided illumination that leaves nothing in shadow. Dickinson was entirely inclined to proclaim the sufficiency of the world: "O Matchless Earth - We underrate the chance to dwell in Thee." And she disclaims the possibility of overturning of any conclusions by countenancing the existence of domains inaccessible to thought:

> I have no Life but this -
> To lead it here -
> Nor any Death - but lest
>
> Dispelled from there -
> Nor tie to Earths to come -
> Nor Action new -
> Except through this Extent -
> The Realm of you -

(Fr 1432c, J 1398; 1877)

I have been primarily talking about the kinds of information we find in poems, cataloguing some typical features we associate with this mode of verbal art: its imaginative mobility, its emphasis on phenomenal states (both conveying information about them and provoking them); its engagement with a present of location; and its interest in totality; and suggesting that all of this creates a pleasing, if slant, rhyme with the contents of the Cosmoscope. In noticing the processes of reasoning taking place within poems, we encounter a rhyme with the *function* of the Cosmoscope. Poems that occupy the

29. John Ashbery, *Self-Portrait in a Convex Mirror* (New York: Viking, 1975), 1.

first person, on this account, are far from being mired in the problems of disclosing personal experience, or of illicitly generalizing from it; rather, they illustrate the role that first-person experience plays in the acquisition of third-person knowledge.

Rhyme, of course, is a certain resemblance, rather than identity. I cannot possibly be saying—can I?—that poems do in fact contain all the relevant information we need to derive the truth about the world; nor can I plausibly defend the often specious reasoning that poems employ to reach their conclusions, whether about God or life or society or beauty or truth. Our poets are as fallible as our statesmen.

For Chalmers, the point, or the promise, of scrutability is not infallibility: it is that "failures of philosophical knowledge can be ascribed either to the non-ideality of our reasoning or to our ignorance of fundamental truths," rather than to some more fatal unknowability of the world.[30] On Chalmers's account—and, I suggest, on Dickinson's account—we have reason to be optimistic about the project and prospects of thinking. Parallels between the work of Cosmoscope and the work of art, then, might encourage us to notice, in case we had forgotten, how often poets understand themselves to be involved in coming to know truths by imaginative means. And they allow us to consider whether the poetic tendency to move from individual experiences to universal conclusions might be a promising (because more comprehensive) way of proceeding.

Finally, to return to my opening considerations, the felicitous rhyme between poetry and the Cosmoscope suggests that certain reductionist ways of dismissing what poems are on about may be wrong. I want to say that if a poem aspires to the condition of the Cosmoscope then poetry aspires to the condition of knowledge. We may disregard the epistemic self-seriousness of the poets and poems

30. Chalmers, *Constructing the World*, xxiii.

as mere vanity, or as ideology; but it would be hard to do so while at the same time claiming to care about these poems. Their urgency in our present moment, as in any present, lies in their pursuit of truth. We may coherently look to them for guidance and hold them to account for failure.[31]

REFERENCES

Adorno, Theodor. "Commitment." *New Left Review* 1, no. 87–88 (1974): 78.

Adorno, Theodor, Gretel Adorno, and Rolf Tiedeman. *Aesthetic Theory*. Theory and History of Literature, vol. 88. Minneapolis: University of Minnesota Press, 1997.

Bacon, Francis. *The Advancement of Learning*. 1st Paul Dry Books Edition. Edited by G. W. Kitchin. Philadelphia: Paul Dry Books, 2000.

Chalmers, David J. "Does Conceivability Entail Possibility?" In *Conceivability and Possibility*, edited by Tamar S. Gendler and John Hawthorne, 145–200. Oxford: Oxford University Press, 2002.

Chalmers, David J. *Constructing the World*. Oxford: Oxford University Press, 2012.

Empson, William. *Milton's God*. London: Chatto & Windus, 1961.

Hume, David. *David Hume: A Treatise of Human Nature: Volume 1: Texts*. Edited by David Fate Norton and Mary J. Norton. Oxford: Clarendon Press, 2007.

Knapp, Steven. *Literary Interest: The Limits of Anti-Formalism*. Cambridge, MA: Harvard University Press, 1993.

Pettit, Philip. "The Possibility of Aesthetic Realism." In *Pleasure, Preference, and Value: Studies in Philosophical Aesthetic*, edited by Eva Schaper, 17–39. Cambridge; New York: Cambridge University Press, 1983.

Yanal, Robert J., ed. *Institutions of Art: Reconsiderations of George Dickie's Philosophy*. University Park: Pennsylvania State University Press, 1994.

31. Thanks to Elisabeth Camp and to all the contributors to this volume for their intellectual generosity and collaborative spirit. Special thanks to Antony Aumann for his pointed and helpful comments on an earlier version of this chapter.

Chapter 4

Form and Content in Emily Dickinson's Poetry

ANTONY AUMANN

ON INTERPRETING POETRY

The aim of this chapter is to reconcile two competing camps of thought about poetry. According to the first camp, there is an intimate relationship between the form and content of many poems. *What* they say is bound up with *how* they say it. As a result, they could not have said what they did in just any old way. According to the second camp, it is possible to paraphrase poems, including the sort just described. We can say what they say in different words. We can even express their content in ordinary and straightforward prose.

We encounter both camps in scholarship on Emily Dickinson's poetry. First, there are those who claim her jarring punctuation, unexpected line breaks, and slant rhymes are crucial for understanding the meaning of her poems. Her unusual formal choices are connected to her challenges to Victorian and Puritan ideas about order, rationality, and tradition. She would have compromised her subversive message

The Poetry of Emily Dickinson. Elisabeth Camp, Oxford University Press (2021). © Oxford University Press.
DOI: 10.1093/oso/9780190651190.003.0005

had she proceeded in a more conventional fashion.[1] Second, there are those who maintain Dickinson's poems are amenable to paraphrase. We can say what she says in other words. In fact, much of the critical literature on Dickinson involves doing precisely that. It expresses in straightforward prose what she expressed in poetry.

In this chapter, I will argue we can embrace both camps. Poems can exhibit *both* unity of form and content *and* paraphrasability. What I say will have broad applicability, but I will focus on Dickinson to make my case. Her poetry is a good test because her form is especially tightly connected to her message. Thus, her poems are especially resistant to paraphrase. Before I turn to Dickinson, however, it is necessary to say more about the two key concepts in play, "unity of form and content" and "paraphrasability."

UNITY OF FORM AND CONTENT

There are at least two ways to understand unity of form and content, a weaker and a stronger way.[2] The stronger way involves taking unity to refer to *inseparability*. A work's form and content are inseparable if we cannot prize them apart without distortion. That is, we cannot understand the content of the work in isolation from the form in

1. See, for example, Budick, *Emily Dickinson and the Life of Language*, 14; Martin, *The Cambridge Introduction to Emily Dickinson*, 33, 41–43; Hagenbüchle, "Precision and Indeterminacy in the Poetry of Emily Dickinson," 50; McIntosh, *Nimble Believing*, 17; Porter, *The Art of Emily Dickinson's Early Poetry*, 119; Ross, "Uncommon Measures: Emily Dickinson's Subversive Prosody," 74, 81, 92; Williams, "Experiments in Poetry: Emily Dickinson," 255.
2. See Schapiro, "On Perfection, Coherence, and Unity of Form and Content," 7–13. Owen Hulatt discusses a third way of understanding unity of form and content. He maintains that unity arises when the form of the poem is unobtrusive. In other words, the poet has executed the formal schema at hand in such a way that it does not feel forced but rather flows organically (Hulatt, "The Problem of Modernism and Critical Refusal: Bradley and Lamarque on Form/Content Unity"). On this account, Dickinson often intentionally breaks with the ideal of unity of form and content.

THE POETRY OF EMILY DICKINSON

which it occurs. Moreover, it is not possible to pair the content with a different form without distorting its meaning.

The weaker way of understanding unity of form and content involves construing unity as *harmony*. [3] The assumption here is that it is possible to distinguish a poem's form and content. Once we distinguish these two elements, we can see them as standing in various relationships with each other. They can complement each other, giving the work a kind of inner harmony. Or, they can fail to fit with each other, creating internal tension and discord.

Harmony between form and content is easier to identify. It can arise in several ways. Perhaps the most obvious is onomatopoeia, a poetic device in which the sound made by uttering the words is connected to the subject matter of the poem. For an example, consider the final line of the first stanza of Dickinson's "A Narrow Fellow in the Grass." The repeated s-sound in "His notice sudden is" resembles the hissing of a snake, which is the poem's subject. [4]

A narrow Fellow in the Grass
Occasionally rides -
You may have met Him - did you not
His notice sudden is -

(F 1096, J 986; 1865)

---

3. Schapiro, "On Perfection, Coherence, and Unity of Form and Content," 7.
4. Not all snakes hiss, of course, but many do, including many New England snakes (Young, "Snake Bioacoustics: Toward a Richer Understanding of the Behavioral Ecology of Snakes"). It is worth adding that Dickinson appears to have been insistent upon the alliteration in this poem. For, in a letter to Thomas Wentworth Higginson, she complained about changes made to it by the *Springfield Daily Republican*. These changes included replacing "sudden" with "instant," which diminishes the alliterative effect. See Denman, "Emily Dickinson's Volcanic Punctuation"; Dickinson and Vendler, *Dickinson*, 399.

FORM AND CONTENT IN EMILY DICKINSON'S POETRY

Form-content harmony has a different basis in "By Homely Gift and Hindered Words." Here the increasingly shorter line lengths reflect the diminution to nothingness that the poem discusses.[5]

> By homely gift and hindered Words
> The human heart is told
> Of Nothing -
>
> (F 1611, J 1563; 1883)

Other rhetorical devices, such as punctuation, can also be used to create inner harmony. For instance, at the end of "After Great Pain, a Formal Feeling Comes," Dickinson employs a series of dashes to slow the tempo. The *ritardando* effect mirrors the experience of freezing described on the semantic level.[6]

> This is the Hour of Lead -
> Remembered, if outlived,
> As Freezing persons, recollected the Snow -
> First - Chill - then Stupor - then the letting go -
>
> (F 372, J 341; 1862)

Thus, we can see how some of Dickinson's poems exhibit unity in the weaker sense of *harmony*. Proving they exhibit unity in the stronger sense of *inseparability* is more difficult. I will attempt the task shortly. But first let me turn to the other main issue in this chapter, paraphrasability.

---

5. Denman, "Emily Dickinson's Volcanic Punctuation," 39.
6. Denman, "Emily Dickinson's Volcanic Punctuation," 27–28; Martin, *The Cambridge Introduction to Emily Dickinson*, 41; Miller, *Emily Dickinson, a Poet's Grammar*, 51.

PARAPHRASABILITY

Paraphrase has been a contentious issue since the rise of New Criticism. It was a dogma of the movement that poems cannot be paraphrased, and at least some opponents have balked at exactly this point.[7] Although the popularity of New Criticism has waned, the battle over paraphrasability is not over. It continues to be attacked and defended on many fronts.[8] Even so, I side with those who think the dispute is largely terminological. It arises because the rival factions do not agree about what paraphrasing involves.[9]

All parties accept that to paraphrase something is to say the same thing in a different way. The question is how to parse "saying the same thing." One option is to construe it broadly. On this view, you manage to say the same thing as someone else only if you produce the same *total effect*. To provide an adequate paraphrase, you must not only express the same propositional content as the other person. You must also capture the emotional power, imagistic force, etc., of his or her words.

Opponents of paraphrase often assume this stringent standard when defending their view. Cleanth Brooks maintained that paraphrases fail because they miss a poem's emotional force.[10] Max Black made the same point when explaining why he thought metaphors resist paraphrase.[11] More recently, Gordon Graham

7. Brooks, "The Heresy of Paraphrase," 192–214. Brooks is responding to Yvor Winters's views, developed among other places in "Primitivism and Decadence: A Study of American Experimental Poetry."
8. See Leighton, "About About: On Poetry and Paraphrase," 168.
9. Cavell, "Aesthetic Problems of Modern Philosophy," 75–76; Kivy, *Philosophies of Arts: An Essay in Differences*, 106; Levinson, "Who's Afraid of a Paraphrase?," 8.
10. Brooks, "The Heresy of Paraphrase," 184; see also Bradley, *Poetry for Poetry's Sake*; Lepore, "The Heresy of Paraphrase," 184–185.
11. Black, "Metaphor," 293; Black, "How Metaphors Work," 141–142; cf. Moran, "Seeing and Believing," 90–94.

has argued paraphrases cannot capture the image provided by a poem.[12] Finally, Angela Leighton has maintained that paraphrases miss the non-propositional element of poems that is central to their significance.[13]

Defenders of paraphrasability, such as Peter Kivy, tend to concede the substantive point here. They allow that our best paraphrases often cannot capture *everything* poems have to offer. What Kivy denies is that paraphrases ought to be able to do such things. The purpose of a paraphrase is not to preserve the total effect of the original poem. It is only to present the poem's propositional content (if the poem has any, and not all poems do).[14]

At this point, a second question arises. Suppose we grant that paraphrasing is only about capturing propositional content. It is still necessary to determine how exhaustively and how precisely this content must be captured. Does an adequate paraphrase have to provide all the propositional content of the original? Or just some? Does it have to convey the exact same propositional content? Or just more or less the same?

Here too opponents of paraphrase often embrace the more restrictive option. For instance, Peter Lamarque claims paraphrases fail because there is no such thing as synonymy at the fine-grained level. Any change in wording—or even in punctuation or grammar—produces a slightly different meaning.[15] Others argue that paraphrases cannot succeed because the meaning of some poems is open-ended. There is no limit to what they suggest and imply, or to what we can

---

12. Graham, "Aesthetic Cognitivism and the Literary Arts," 3.

13. Leighton, "About About," 170–171.

14. Camp, "Metaphor and That Certain 'Je Ne Sais Quoi,'" 2; Kivy, *Philosophies of Arts*, 104–106.

15. Lamarque, "Poetry and Abstract Thought," 46; Lamarque, "The Elusiveness of Poetic Meaning," 398–420; and Lamarque, "Semantic Finegrainedness and Poetic Value," 24–28.

get out of them. Thus, it is simply impossible to say everything these poems say.[16]

Once again, defenders of paraphrase tend to concede the substance of the opponent's position. A paraphrase may not be able to capture all or exactly the propositional content of a poem. Especially if this includes all the propositions the poem might bring to mind. But defenders of paraphrase counter by saying the bar should not be set so high. Success should not require reproducing every statement a poem might be taken to say or to imply. Nor should it require doing so with perfect precision. The reason for lowering the bar here is that a paraphrase is not supposed to be a *substitute* for the original.[17] As Brooks himself concedes, it is only supposed to be a "scaffolding" that helps us understand the original.[18] A paraphrase only has to say more or less what the original poem says on one interpretation to serve this purpose.

In this chapter, I will adopt this final, modest view of paraphrase. I will hold that an adequate paraphrase only has to capture the propositional content and not the total effect of the poem. In addition, it does not have to reproduce all the propositional content. It only has to present approximately what the work says on one acceptable interpretation.

16. For discussion of this point, see Black, "More about Metaphor," 443–445; Black, "How Metaphors Work," 142; Camp, "Metaphor and That Certain 'Je Ne Sais Quoi,'" 6–8; Cavell, "Aesthetic Problems of Modern Philosophy," 79; Davidson, "What Metaphors Mean," 46n16; Hills, "Problems of Paraphrase: Bottom's Dream," 31.

17. Bache, "Paraphrase and Paraphrasing Metaphors"; Black, "How Metaphors Work," 142; Cavell, "Aesthetic Problems of Modern Philosophy," 75; Kivy, *Philosophies of Arts*, 105–106.

18. Brooks, "The Heresy of Paraphrase," 182; Kivy, "Paraphrasing Poetry (for Profit and Pleasure).".

THE TENSION BETWEEN PARAPHRASABILITY
AND UNITY OF FORM AND CONTENT

We can now return to the questions raised at the outset of the chapter. Is paraphrasability consistent with unity of form and content? Can a particular poem exhibit both of these features?

At first pass, the answer seems to depend on how we think about unity of form and content. If we interpret unity in the weaker way as *harmony*, the two theses appear consistent. The inner harmony of a poem may be hard to capture in a paraphrase. But harmony tends to contribute to a poem's total effect, not its propositional content. Since a paraphrase only has to capture propositional content, the fact that a poem exhibits harmony of form and content will not make it resistant to paraphrase.

Think again about Dickinson's "After Great Pain, a Formal Feeling Comes." It possesses inner harmony because the slowing of the cadence brought about by the introduction of dashes corresponds to the experience of freezing to death that the poem describes. The coincidence of sound and sense is pleasing to the ear and makes the poem memorable. But it does not express some new claim about the subject matter of the poem. Thus, a paraphrase does not have to capture it.[19]

Matters are different if we interpret unity in the stronger way as *inseparability*. Now unity does seem inconsistent with paraphrasability. If the form and content of a poem are inseparable, we cannot

---

19. Moreover, even if the inner harmony of the poem *did* assert some new claim, it would not necessarily be a problem. For there is no *prima facie* reason the new claim could not be expressed straightforwardly in a paraphrase. For instance, suppose the slowing of the cadence at the end of "After Great Pain, A Formal Feeling Comes" asserted the point that freezing to death involved a slowing of the mind. It would not be difficult to include this point as part of the paraphrase. This point is made by Ernie Lepore. See "The Heresy of Paraphrase," 177–197; "Poetry, Medium and Message."

change the form without distorting the content. Yet, a paraphrase necessarily involves changing the form; for a paraphrase is an attempt to say the same thing *in a different way*. So, it seems a paraphrase necessarily involves distorting the content. Of course, not every paraphrase will distort the content so much that it fails even approximately to capture the meaning of the original. But this will be a constant danger.

The rest of this chapter will focus on the tension between paraphrasability and unity-as-inseparability. I will argue that it is possible to resolve this tension. My strategy will be to examine why inseparability arises when it does. I believe once we understand the source of inseparability, we will be able to see why it is consistent with paraphrasability after all. A close look at Dickinson's works will guide us along the way.

UNITY OF FORM AND CONTENT IN DICKINSON'S POETRY

Dickinson scholars often praise her poetry because it exhibits unity of form and content in the weaker sense of *harmony*. Her unorthodox punctuation, meter, and rhyme schemes fit well with her unorthodox ideas. For example, Stanley Williams writes, "In her half-rhymes, her irregularities of speech and rhythm, her spasmodic quality, she mirrored the incongruities and frustrations of human experience; the awkwardness in her poetry became a metaphor of life itself."[20] In Miller Budick's words, "Disorder, therefore, is conveyed in Dickinson's poetry not only imagistically and thematically. It is represented linguistically and visually as well."[21] Finally,

---

20. Williams, "Experiments in Poetry: Emily Dickinson," 255; see also Porter, *The Art of Emily Dickinson's Early Poetry*, 119.
21. Budick, *Emily Dickinson and the Life of Language*, 14.

as James McIntosh puts it, Dickinson's greatness lay in her ability to find "appropriate styles and forms for representing an untethered inner life."[22]

Yet, some scholars make the stronger claim that the form and content of Dickinson's poems are *inseparable*. For instance, Wendy Martin says Dickinson *had* to express her subversive views in an unconventional form. "She abandoned standard meter and rhyme, threw conventional grammar out the window, and forced her readers to work to understand her meaning. *The traditional structures of poetry were incapable of conveying the ideas she wanted to express.*"[23] Roland Hagenbüchle makes a similar point. He asserts, "Emily Dickinson's poetry is characterized by an element of deliberate indeterminacy, *which alone can do justice to the mystery of existence.*"[24] Such thoughts give rise to Sharon Leiter's thesis that Dickinson's works defy paraphrase.

> "Where paraphrase is possible," wrote the great 20th-century Russian poet Osip Mandelstam, "the sheets have not been rumpled. Poetry has not spent the night." Anyone who has attempted to paraphrase a Dickinson poem, to reduce it to a simple clean thought, knows that her sheets are indeed rumpled.[25]

I am inclined to agree with Martin, Hagenbüchle, and Leiter. It seems right to say Dickinson had to write how she did. A conventional approach would have compromised her anti-conventional

22. McIntosh, *Nimble Believing*, 17.
23. Martin, *The Cambridge Introduction to Emily Dickinson*, 33, emphasis added; see also Martin, *The Cambridge Introduction to Emily Dickinson*, 41–43; Ross, "Uncommon Measures," 74, 81, 92; Leiter, *Critical Companion to Emily Dickinson*, xi.
24. Hagenbüchle, "Precision and Indeterminacy in the Poetry of Emily Dickinson," 50, emphasis added.
25. Leiter, *Critical Companion to Emily Dickinson*, xi.

message. Yet, it is not exactly clear why, and Martin *et alia* do not say. So what we need is an argument.

One possible starting point is Martha Nussbaum's idea that form is not always neutral.[26] Form can shape and condition content. More importantly, form can contribute to content. Using a particular form can express judgments and claims; it can imply the acceptance or rejection of a particular worldview. From Nussbaum's idea, it follows that the form of a poem can stand in various logical relationships to its content. In particular, the form can be logically consistent or logically inconsistent with the content. The claims implied by the form can fit with the poem's intended message or conflict with it.[27]

Inconsistencies or conflicts between form and content hold the key to *inseparability*. To see why, think about the impact of form-content conflicts on ordinary conversation. Imagine a person who terminated a spat with you by repeatedly yelling, "I don't care what you think about me!" In such a situation, we might wonder whether the person believed the content of his or her outburst. If they did not care, why are they yelling? Or, suppose someone said to you, "A person ought to use gender-neutral language in his speech." Here it would be reasonable to doubt whether the person grasped what he or she was saying. If the person stood behind gender-neutral language, why use masculine pronouns when referring to a person in the abstract?

In sum, conflicts between form and content in ordinary conversation generate incoherence. They make us confused about what people are trying to say and make us doubt whether people stand behind their utterances. This point applies to poetry as well. If poets use a

---

26. Nussbaum, "Form and Content, Philosophy and Literature," in *Love's Knowledge*, 15; see also Aumann, "The Relationship between Aesthetic Value and Cognitive Value," 117–127; Brooks, "The Heresy of Paraphrase," 180; Lepore, "The Heresy of Paraphrase," 196–197.
27. For development of this idea, see Aumann, "The Relationship between Aesthetic Value and Cognitive Value."

form that is inconsistent with their message, they undercut them-selves. They prevent themselves from successfully communicating with their readers and listeners. We can derive a rule about insepara-bility from this observation. *The content of a poem is inseparable from the forms in which it can be consistently expressed.*

For an example of how this rule works, we can think about Dickinson's relationship to hymn form. Hymn form refers to 4-3-4-3 or "common" meter combined with iambic stresses and an *abcb* rhyme scheme. The lines are also usually end-stopped rather than enjambed.[28] Hymn form dominated Puritan church music in the seventeenth through nineteenth centuries.[29] In particular, it was the form used by Isaac Watts, whose hymnals were everywhere in New England, including the Dickinson home.[30] Because of hymn form's prevalence in the Puritan church, it came to be associated with Puritan views. The association was so strong that using hymn form came to imply support for Puritan ways of thinking.

Like all citizens of mid-nineteenth century Amherst, Dickinson imbibed the Puritan tradition. Her poems often traded in Puritan ideas and made use of Puritan imagery. Yet, although she sometimes seems obsessed with hymn form, she frequently departs from it.[31] She often abandons 4-3-4-3 measure and its variants, whereas Watts almost never did.[32] She also more freely uses false rhymes than Watts, who felt the need to make his rhymes exact, especially at the end of

---

28. England, "Emily Dickinson and Isaac Watts," 130n29; Johnson, *Emily Dickinson: An Interpretive Biography*, 85; Lindberg-Seyersted, *The Voice of the Poet: Aspects of Style in the Poetry of Emily Dickinson*, 156.
29. England, "Emily Dickinson and Isaac Watts," 130n29; Porter, *The Art of Emily Dickinson's Early Poetry*, 56.
30. Miller, "Dickinson's Structured Rhythms," 394–395; Porter, *The Art of Emily Dickinson's Early Poetry*, 74.
31. England, "Emily Dickinson and Isaac Watts," 131; Porter, *The Art of Emily Dickinson's Early Poetry*, 55; cf. Small, *Positive as Sound: Emily Dickinson's Rhyme* (University of Georgia Press, 2010), 41–48.
32. England, "Emily Dickinson and Isaac Watts," 130n30.

his hymns.[33] Finally, unlike Watts, Dickinson does not always end-stop her lines but makes use of enjambment. In fact, she frequently does not even end her lines as the meter demands. She pushes the final word or phrase to the following line where it stands alone.[34]

Why did Dickinson *have to* write this way? The reason, I maintain, is that she was not an unwavering supporter of Puritan ways. She challenged and questioned them as often as she affirmed them. Thus, a sincere and unwavering adherence to hymn form would have been inappropriate. It would have implied a greater allegiance to the Puritan worldview than she actually held. In sum, Dickinson had to write how she did because logical consistency demanded it. She had to depart from hymn form at least some of the time because she would have contradicted herself had she not.

We can see a second example of inseparability of form and content if we look at Dickinson's attitude toward the poetics defended by Henry Home, Lord Kames. In his *Elements of Criticism*, Kames asserts that the meter and rhyme of a poem should be regularized and "subjected to certain inflexible laws."[35] Grammatical and punctuation rules ought to be observed. In addition, congruence of line and thought breaks is mandatory. Kames writes, "As in general, there ought to be a strict concordance between a thought and the words in which it is dressed; so in particular, every close in the sense ought to be accompanied with a close in the sound."[36]

---

33. England, "Emily Dickinson and Isaac Watts," 129; Miller, *Emily Dickinson, a Poet's Grammar*, 142.
34. England, "Emily Dickinson and Isaac Watts," 130.
35. Kames, *Elements of Criticism*, 2:440.
36. Kames, *Elements of Criticism*, 2005, 2:447. Later, Kames adds: "This sets the matter in a clear light; for, as observed above, a musical pause is intimately connected with a pause in the sense, and ought, as far as possible, to be governed by it: particularly a musical pause ought never to be placed where a pause is excluded by the sense" (*Elements of Criticism*, 2005, 2:467).

Kames defends his view on empiricist grounds. Following Hume, he draws on his own experiences and felt responses to things.[37] He regards order and regularity as beautiful because they feel pleasant to him.[38] By contrast, he downgrades disorder and discord because they strike him as unpleasant.[39] Kames admits he is appealing to his own tastes here.[40] But he does not think his tastes are subjective. At least not in the sense of being idiosyncratic or arbitrary. He considers his tastes to be the product of his rational human nature.[41] They reveal a "universal standard" that strikes him as "perfect or right."[42] In the end, although Kames is an empiricist, he maintains that art is a "rational science" governed by "rational principles."[43] And one of these rational principles is the traditional idea that, insofar as an artwork aims at beauty, it ought to exhibit order and regularity.[44]

Kames's *Elements* was widely read in nineteenth-century America. Dickinson in particular was familiar with it. She had studied Kames during her time at Mount Holyoke and there was a copy of the *Elements* in the family library. It is no surprise that Dickinson may have been positively influenced by Kames in some respects, as Eleanor Heginbotham argues.[45] But Dickinson did not agree with Kames on all points. In particular, she rejected the tight connection he drew between beauty and order. This connection did not fit her

37. Kames, *Elements of Criticism*, 1:262; Kivy, "Lord Kames and the Sense of Beauty"; Stolnitz, "'Beauty': Some Stages in the History of an Idea," 195–196.

38. Kames, *Elements of Criticism*, 2005, 1:141–149. In general, Kames says, "With regard to objects of sight, whatever gives pleasure, is said to be beautiful; whatever gives pain, is said to be ugly" (*Essays on the Principles of Morality and Natural Religion*, 30).

39. Kames, *Elements of Criticism*, 2005, 2:445–446.

40. Kames, *Elements of Criticism*, 2005, 1:141, 2:460.

41. Kames, *Elements of Criticism*, 2005, 2:721–722; Guyer, *Values of Beauty*, 65.

42. Kames, *Elements of Criticism*, 2005, 1:79, 2:722.

43. Kames, *Elements of Criticism*, 2005, 1:14, 1:16, 2:248.

44. Kames, *Elements of Criticism*, 2005, 1:27, 1:141–149; 2:722; see England, "Emily Dickinson and Isaac Watts," 140–142; Ross, "Uncommon Measures," 76, 81–82.

45. Heginbotham, *Reading the Fascicles of Emily Dickinson*, 18–20.

experience. She saw the world as full of chaos and disorder, but no less beautiful because of it. This is not to say that Dickinson regarded order as bad or ugly. It is just to say that, unlike Kames, she saw goodness and beauty in disorder as well.[46]

In sum, Dickinson rejected Kames's rationalist view of art. As such, following his rigid principles would not have made sense for her. In fact, it would have been misleading. It would have suggested acceptance of the very ideology she rejected. Thus, consistency required Dickinson to depart from Kames's poetics. She had to use what would have been for Kames non-standard meter, punctuation, rhyme scheme, and the like.[47]

This account helps explain what we find in Dickinson's poems. Although they adhere to Kames's rules in some respects, they often do not. We encounter jarring punctuation and unexpected line breaks as well as slant rhymes and offbeat meter. These features led some early critics to lament that she was ignorant of the tradition. Others complained she did not understand the rational basis for poetry or needed a lesson in basic grammar.[48] By my lights, these critics have it wrong. Dickinson did not accidently transgress accepted poetic standards because she was unfamiliar with them. She violated them because she understood them and disagreed with them. Her non-traditional poetics was a consequence of defiance, not ignorance.

This point also helps explain why Dickinson was such a great poet. She may not have been the first to challenge Puritan ideas or rational ways of thinking about art. But she was one of the first to recognize

46. Martin, *The Cambridge Introduction to Emily Dickinson*, 41.
47. Ross, "Uncommon Measures," 81. In one sense, Dickinson does not depart from Kames. She still abides by his central principle that form must fit content (Kames, *Elements of Criticism*, 2005, 386).
48. Blackmur, "Emily Dickinson: Notes on Prejudice and Fact," in *The Recognition of Emily Dickinson*, 223; Higginson, "Preface to Poems by Emily Dickinson," 12; Monro, "Emily Dickinson—Overrated," 121.

the implications of these challenges. She saw that traditional ways of thinking were connected to traditional ways of writing poetry. Thus, protesting the former required departing from the latter. This insight led her to write more consistent and thus more powerful poems.

It is worth noting that my view does *not* entail all protests of tradition must occur in a non-traditional poetic form. The requirement of a non-standard form arises only in contexts where a standard form would imply allegiance to the tradition one wished to protest. For example, today we do not associate Puritan ideas or rational views of art with any particular poetic form. Thus, it is possible for us to express our criticisms of these ideas in any way we see fit. We could even express them in traditional hymn form without contradicting ourselves. I will return to this point later.

CASE STUDY: "I FELT A FUNERAL, IN MY BRAIN"

I have been arguing in an abstract way that Dickinson's poetry exhibits inseparability of form and content. I now wish to examine a concrete case. Several of Dickinson's poems would do. But one representative example is "I Felt a Funeral, in My Brain" (F 340, J 280; 1862).[49]

> I felt a Funeral, in my Brain,
> And Mourners to and fro
> Kept treading - treading - till it seemed
> That Sense was breaking through -
> And when they all were seated,

---

49. For other examples, see "The Mountains Stood in Haze" (F 1225, J 1278, 1873) as discussed by Lindberg-Seyersted, *The Voice of the Poet*, 166–167; "Heaven - Is What I Cannot Reach" (F 310, J 239, 1862) as discussed by Porter, *The Art of Emily Dickinson's Early Poetry*, 117–118; and, finally, "You're Right - The Way is Narrow" (F 249, J 234, 1861) as discussed by England, "Emily Dickinson and Isaac Watts," 135–136.

A Service, like a Drum -
Kept beating - beating - till I thought
My mind was going numb -
And then I heard them lift a Box
And creak across my Soul
With those same Boots of Lead, again,
Then Space - began to toll,
As all the Heavens were a Bell,
And Being, but an Ear,
And I, and Silence, some strange Race
Wrecked, solitary, here -
And then a Plank in Reason, broke,
And I dropped down, and down -
And hit a World, at every plunge,
And Finished knowing - then -

On the semantic level, the poem describes some kind of mental breakdown.[50] The exact occasion is unclear. Whatever it is—perhaps an actual death?[51]—the fallout is traumatic enough to be likened to a funeral. The trauma is compounded by social pressures. The fact that it is churchgoers ("Mourners"), pall-bearers (those who "lift a Box"), and a funeral service itself that

---

50. Dickinson and Vendler, *Dickinson*, 141; Reynolds, "Emily Dickinson and Popular Culture," 180–181; Sewall, *The Life of Emily Dickinson*, vol. 2, 502.

51. Some argue that "I Felt a Funeral in My Brain" cannot literally be about a funeral because literal funerals do not take place in literal brains. (See, for example, Cameron, *Lyric Time*, 96–97, and *Choosing Not Choosing*, 142–143.) This view misinterprets the opening line. The poet is not telling us where the funeral takes place. She is telling us where she *felt* the funeral. More precisely, she is telling us where she felt her emotional responses to the funeral. And where else could she feel these responses than her brain? For other interpretations of this poem, Dickinson and Vendler, *Dickinson*, 141–143; Karen Jackson Ford, *Gender and the Poetics of Excess: Moments of Brocade* (University Press of Mississippi, 2011), 68–70; Reynolds, "Emily Dickinson and Popular Culture," 180; Sewall, *The Life of Emily Dickinson*, 2:502–503; Wolff, *Emily Dickinson*, 227–233.

oppress her—maybe even a preacher's voice[52]—suggests that perhaps a religious ideology is being forced upon her. The reference to a drum beat, the repeated words ("beating - Beating," "treading - treading), as well as the successive "and's" hint that maybe orderliness and regularity are being pushed upon her too. As the assault continues, her head starts ringing. So much so that it feels as if her entire body is an ear and the world around her is a tolling bell. She cannot find a way to quiet her troubled mind, coming up short in her pursuit of silence. Finally, she gives out. Her way of thinking—her own "plank of Reason"—collapses under the external pressure. The result is that the poet is lost. She cannot understand anything anymore. Thus, we are led to infer that what the churchgoers and preacher are offering is an inadequate substitute for her own thinking. They may have promised knowledge and comprehension. Indeed, "Sense" seemed to break through when they first set upon her. But they do not deliver in the end.

The poem adheres to Watts's hymn form in some respects but not others. It uses common meter throughout. Apart from the last line of the third stanza, which was the conclusion of the poem in its initial printing, it exhibits iambic stresses. The poem also follows the standard *abcb* rhyme scheme. The middle three stanzas use exact rhymes; the first and last employ slant rhymes. Finally, the poem's punctuation is grammatically nonstandard. Periods have been omitted. The commas and dashes serve rhetorical rather than grammatical or semantic purposes.[53]

The poem's form mirrors its semantic content in several ways. The inconsistent use of hymn form suggests an uncertain attitude toward Puritan ways of thinking. The frequent departures from regimented

---

52. Dickinson and Vendler, *Dickinson*, 142.
53. Miller, *Emily Dickinson, a Poet's Grammar*, 53.

prosody imply a similarly equivocal attitude toward the Kamesian views about order and regularity that lie behind them. In addition, the fact that the most remarkable departures from traditional form occur at the end—the jarring slant rhyme in the last stanza (down/then) and the trochaic rather than iambic feet in the last line—hints that the poet's final attitude regarding traditional views is negative. Puritan approaches to life and orderly ways of viewing the world do not work for her.[54]

Such unity of form and content is an aesthetic virtue. It is part of what makes the poem great. But there is more to the matter. Dickinson did not align the poem's form and content just out of concern for poetic excellence. It was also a matter of necessity. Dickinson *had to* write more or less how she did to express the poem's message. She *had to* break in some way from hymn form and from rationalist prosodics. For if she had not—if she had perfectly conformed to Kames's prosodics and perfectly followed Watts's hymn form—she would have tacitly endorsed both Kamesian and Puritan ways of thinking. But these ways of thinking are what she wished to call into question. They are what she found inadequate to the task of making sense of the world. Thus, an unqualified adherence to hymn form or Kamesian prosodics would not just have been an aesthetic defect. It would not just have meant a displeasing loss of harmony between form and content. It would also have resulted in a performative contradiction. Dickinson would have affirmed in how she wrote the worldview she challenged in what she wrote.

To support the claim that stylistic conformity would have created deep problems in "I Felt a Funeral, in My Brain," we can

54. Miles, "The Irregularities of Emily Dickinson," 123–129; Miller, *Emily Dickinson, a Poet's Grammar*, 116; Porter, *The Art of Emily Dickinson's Early Poetry*, 118; Ross, "Uncommon Measures," 81–82; cf. Allen, "Emily Dickinson's Versification," in *The Recognition of Emily Dickinson*, 182–183.

look at a similar poem, "I Felt a Cleaving In My Mind" (F 867, J 937; 1864):

> I felt a Cleaving in my Mind -
> As if my Brain had split -
> I tried to match it - Seam by Seam -
> But could not make them fit -
> The thought behind, I strove to join
> Unto the thought before
> But Sequence raveled out of Sound -
> Like Balls - upon a Floor -

In terms of content, this poem expresses the same kind of mental breakdown encountered in "I Felt a Funeral, in My Brain." It articulates the same kind of inability of the author to make sense of something in an orderly or rational fashion. Yet, it does not similarly depart from hymn form. It unswervingly follows the 4-3-4-3 beat structure of common meter, and it does not deviate from the standard *abcb* rhyme scheme. It even makes uses of exact rhymes (split/fit; before/Floor). The result is disruptive to the coherence of the poem. The regular rhythm and rhyme give the poem a light and happy feeling, which belies the seriousness of its content. The orderly prosody suggests the poet is capable of orderly thinking after all. In sum, Dickinson's choice of form in this poem undermines and contradicts the message she is trying to convey.

Note that my argument here does not establish the necessity of *the specific form* of "I Felt a Funeral in My Brain." It does not show Dickinson had to use a non-standard metrical foot at the end of the fourth stanza or a slant rhyme at the end of the fifth stanza. The argument's conclusion is merely that Dickinson had to depart *in some way or other* from hymn form and rationalist prosodics. She had to use *some kind* of non-conventional format. Not necessarily the particular one she did.

PARAPHRASING DICKINSON

The central question of this chapter is whether unity of form and content is consistent with paraphrasability. In other words, can a poem exhibit both of these properties? In the preceding sections, I argued that some of Dickinson's poems exhibit unity. Thus, the question now becomes whether these poems are also paraphrasable. Can we express their propositional content in straightforward and literal prose?

I think the answer to this question is yes. We *can* paraphrase Dickinson's poems. Critics and commentators do it all the time. Indeed, my discussion of "I Felt a Funeral, in My Brain" included a partial paraphrase. What is perplexing is how this could be so. How could it be that *Dickinson* had to express her unconventional ideas in an unconventional format, but *we critics* can convey the same ideas straightforwardly? How could it be that there are constraints on her form of expression but not ours? It seems one of these two ideas must go. If we want to hold on to paraphrasability, we should concede Dickinson could have expressed herself in any old way. If we wish to insist Dickinson had to express herself how she did, we should concede a paraphrase somehow comes up short.

There are a few tempting ways to respond to this dilemma. The first is to say Dickinson faced stylistic restrictions because of the historical context in which she wrote. In nineteenth-century New England, the expression of religious ideas may have frequently occurred through hymn form. So then and there the use of hymn form may have implied support for religious ways of thinking. But we do not make these associations any more. Hymn form has long been divorced from religious content. Poets now use it to express all kinds of other things as well. Thus, the implications and restrictions Dickinson had to deal with do not apply to us today.

There is something to this first line of response. The implications that attach to a particular form often arise because of conventional associations. As a result, when these conventions disappear, so too do the implications. Yet, this point does not explain why Dickinson faced stylistic restrictions but critics do not. For it does not accommodate the intuition that a critic who lived in Dickinson's time and place could have paraphrased her poems. Thomas Wentworth Higginson, for instance, could have supplied a gloss of the poems he published in the *Springfield Daily Republican* in the 1860s. At least, it would not have been incoherent for him to do so.

The second temptation is to say Dickinson faced stylistic restrictions because she was writing poetry and not prose. It might be reasonable in a poetic context to hold that employing a given form implies claims. But the idea seems less plausible in the context of discussing prose. When writing in a particular prose style, we tend not to think we are declaring our allegiance to some ideology. When reading the prose of others—especially if it is academic prose—we rarely consider whether their form implies commitments or claims. Thus, perhaps prose is different from poetry in being unburdened by implications.

I do not think this view of prose is accurate, and I have argued against it elsewhere.[55] More importantly, Dickinson rejects the view. Prose writing has a robust set of connotations in her mind. She associates it with limitation and restriction. In particular, she connected it with the suppression of her voice and perspective. For example, in "They Shut Me Up in Prose" (F 445, J 613, 1862), she links prose with her experience as a child of having been confined to a closet. In "I Dwell in Possibility" (F 466, J 657, 1862), she likens poetry to a house that is more open and expansive than the house of prose. Finally, in a note to her sister-in-law, Susan Dickinson, she expresses

---

55. Aumann, "The Relationship between Aesthetic Value and Cognitive Value."

THE POETRY OF EMILY DICKINSON

her high estimation of their creative abilities by saying, "we are the only poets, and everyone else is *prose*."[56]

Thus, Dickinson did not face stylistic restrictions because she wrote poetry rather than prose. She would have faced restrictions on the prose front as well. Since she believed prose implied restrictiveness, it would have been wrong to use prose to pursue her ideal of "circumference"—the project of "embracing life with the most complete and comprehensive perspective."[57] We see this fact borne out in her letters. Personal correspondence would ordinarily be an occasion for prose. But Dickinson's correspondence contains poetic elements, including meter, rhyme, and line breaks. Parts have even been published as poetry.[58]

Although these two tempting responses fail, they are on the right track. There is a difference between what Dickinson is doing qua poet and what we are doing qua critics. But the difference is not that we are writing in different genres or historical contexts. It is that we are performing different types of speech acts. Poets are doing something akin to assertion. They are presenting their own views, perspectives, and attitudes about some subject matter. By contrast, when we critics are paraphrasing poets, we are engaging in reported speech. We are conveying what someone else has said rather than expressing positions of our own. These two speech acts—assertion and reported speech—are governed by different norms. Thus, they are encumbered with different restrictions. Let me explain.

An assertion is an utterance in which we claim something holds or is true. It follows that, when making one, we represent ourselves

56. Dickinson, *The Letters of Emily Dickinson*, 144, L56. For other discussions, see Barker, "Emily Dickinson and Poetic Strategy," 78; Ross, "Uncommon Measures," 72; Miller, *Emily Dickinson, a Poet's Grammar*, 145–147.

57. Martin, *The Cambridge Introduction to Emily Dickinson*, 34.

58. Erkkila, "The Emily Dickinson Wars," 18; Spicer, "The Poems of Emily Dickinson".

as standing behind what we are saying.[59] We commit ourselves to the accuracy of our statement.[60] For example, if I say, "death defies rational comprehension," I commit myself to the view that death defies rational comprehension.

Reported speech is different. When paraphrasing or quoting someone, we may represent ourselves as standing behind the accuracy of our report. We may commit ourselves to having captured what the original speaker said. Thus, there is a sense in which we are making a kind of assertion. Yet, in reported speech, we do not represent ourselves as believing the content of the original speaker's utterance. We do not commit ourselves to the truth of what the original speaker said. For example, if I state that, "Dickinson said that death defies rational comprehension," I do not represent myself as standing behind the idea that death defies rational comprehension. I attribute this idea to Dickinson. Of course, I may agree with her. But such agreement is not implied by my report of her words.

The fact that in assertions we stand behind what we are saying whereas in reported speech we do not has an important consequence. It entails form-content contradictions can plague assertions but not reported speech. Let me explain why.

In the case of an assertion, a form-content contradiction undermines the speaker's reliability. Because the form of the speaker's utterance implies something that conflicts with the content of the utterance, it calls into question whether the speaker believes the content. It suggests the speaker may not understand what he or she is saying or may not stand behind it. In either case, there is reason to question the speaker's assertion.

59. Searle, *Speech Acts*, 64, 66; Bach and Harnish, *Linguistic Communication and Speech Acts*, 42; Williams, *Truth and Truthfulness*, 74.
60. Peirce, "Judgment and Assertion," 385–387.

Form-content contradictions do not threaten the reliability of someone who reports the speech of another. If a person uses a form that contradicts the content he or she is reporting, this may suggest he or she does not believe the content. But it will not thereby impugn his or her epistemic standing. For a person does not represent himself or herself as believing the content he or she is simply reporting.

An example illustrates the point:

JOHN: A person should use gender-neutral language in his speech.

JANE: According to John, a person should use gender-neutral language in his speech.

The form of John's assertion contradicts its content. His decision to use a masculine pronoun rather than an available neutral term to refer to a speaker in the abstract implies he thinks gendered language is acceptable.[61] Yet, this is the opposite of what he says. Thus, a question arises as to whether John stands behind his assertion and grasps the import of it. Jane's utterance does not suffer from this problem. She also uses a masculine pronoun when referring to a speaker in the abstract. This may signify that she too considers gendered language permissible. But even so, Jane does not thereby contradict herself. For she does not represent herself as believing John's claim that speakers ought to use gender-neutral language. She merely attributes the claim to him.

We can apply this lesson to the case of Emily Dickinson. If Dickinson wishes to assert a challenge to Puritan ideals in one of her poems, she must use a form that fits this challenge. In particular, she must not use a form, such as hymn form, that would signify

61. Bolinger, "The Pragmatics of Slurs."

support for Puritan ideals. Doing so would imply acceptance of what she wants to question, and so amount to a performative contradiction. Critics intent on paraphrasing Dickinson are not similarly constrained. They can use whatever form they like to report her challenge to Puritanism. By making such a report, they do not represent themselves as endorsing the challenge. So, they do not call their own reliability into question if they use a form that supports Puritan ways.

To summarize, form-content contradictions can plague assertions but not reported speech. So, when a poet such as Dickinson asserts something, she must use a form that fits her content. By contrast, when reporting a poet's attitudes and beliefs, critics face no such restriction. They do not have to use a form that fits their content. This is the sense in which form and content can be inseparable for the poet but not for the critic.[62]

THE CONVERSATION MODEL
OF INTERPRETATION

A central part of my view is that Dickinson is doing something akin to making assertions. She is setting forth ideas as right or true. She is representing herself as standing behind or endorsing what she says. As a result, her poems contain statements of her beliefs. This is a version of Noël Carroll's conversational model of interpretation. According to Carroll, when interpreting a work of art, we should

---

62. We might wonder what happens if the critic does not just report but actually endorses the poet's ideas. In some such cases, the upshot will be that the critic is subject to the same constraints as the poet. But not always. The critic may live in a different historical context governed by different conventions. If so, the critic will not face the same constraints as the poet. This explains our present situation. The scholarly world is no longer dominated by Kames's view of art. Thus, agreeing with Dickinson's criticisms of Kames would not require us to follow her style.

think of ourselves as engaged in a conversation with the artist. Our task is to figure out what the artist is trying to say to us through his or her work.[63]

There are several ways to challenge my approach here. First, Dickinson often does not seem to be making assertions in her poetry. She seems to be forwarding hypotheses, making conjectures, or simply offering memorable sequences of words, as Jonathan Culler suggests.[64] Thus, she is not presenting the statements we encounter as right or true. She is presenting them as plausible, interesting, or otherwise worthy of our attention. As such, we should not think she believes everything she says. We should allow that she might have doubts about much of what she writes down. One benefit of this interpretation is that it explains why her poetry contains so many contradictions. It is not because she embraces inconsistency or does not understand rudimentary logic. It is because she wants to investigate or experiment with alternative ways of thinking about her subject matter.

If Dickinson's poetry does not contain assertions, then the worry about form-content contradictions disappears. Even if Dickinson uses a form that conflicts with the content of a poem, it does not undermine her epistemic standing. Of course, it might still lead us to question whether she believes what the poem says. But it does not cast doubt on her sincerity or reliability. For she does not represent herself as believing what the poem says. Once the threat of form-content contradictions goes by the board, my argument collapses. There is no longer reason to think her form must fit her content. She can express her ideas however she pleases.

In response, I concede we should not always interpret Dickinson's poems as containing assertions. Culler is right that she sometimes

63. Carroll, "Art, Intention, and Conversation."
64. Culler, *Theory of the Lyric*, 109–131.

engages in speech acts that do not involve standing behind what she says. But I do not think we should totally abandon the idea that her poems contain statements of her beliefs. Doing so would make nonsense out of a common practice. Scholars often treat Dickinson's poetry as if it expressed her views. They support their claims that she held a particular belief by quoting or paraphrasing one or more of her poems. If her poems did not contain assertions, if they did not present views she stood behind, this practice would be misguided. The content of her poetry would provide no evidence that she embraced or rejected a particular position. Of course, some scholars might accept this implication. I do not. I believe our interpretive principles generally ought to accord with how we actually proceed. Maintaining that our customary practices sometimes go astray is fine. Holding that we err systematically is a *reductio ad absurdum*.

There is a second way to challenge my application of the conversational model of interpretation to Dickinson's poetry. Even when it does seem best to read her poems as containing assertions, it is not clear we should attribute these assertions to her. For she may not be speaking in her own voice when she writes. Like an actor on the stage, she may be taking on a persona. She may be occupying a character who is performing a speech act, not performing one herself. So, just as we do not attribute to an actor the claims he or she makes on the stage, so too we should not attribute to Dickinson the claims found in her poems.[65] Indeed, there is good reason to think this approach is correct. In one of her letters to Higginson, Dickinson explicitly says she does not speak in her own voice in her poetry. She writes, "When I state myself, as the representative of the verse, it does not mean me, but a supposed person."[66]

65. See Beardsley, "Intentions and Interpretations: A Fallacy Revisited"; Carroll, "Art, Intention, and Conversation," 103–106; Nathan, "Art, Meaning, and Artist's Meaning," 287.
66. Dickinson, *The Letters of Emily Dickinson*, 412, L268; Martin, *The Cambridge Introduction to Emily Dickinson*, 49.

I believe we ought to take Dickinson at her word here. We should allow that some of the time she is not speaking in her own voice. Yet, the relationship between form and content remains important in these situations. If Dickinson does not speak in her own voice in a given poem, using an inconsistent form does not undermine her epistemic standing. But it does undermine the standing of the "supposed person" in whose voice she is speaking. Returning to the example of an actor on the stage helps here. Suppose while portraying a petulant teenager, an actor screams at the other characters, "I don't care what any of you think about me!" Uttering this line in this way does not prompt us to question *the actor's* state of mind. But it does make us wonder about the mindset of *the character* whom the actor is playing. The intensity with which the claim is expressed suggests the character wants to get it across. Yet, the desire to get the message across makes sense only if he or she cares what the other characters think. And that is the opposite of what he or she says. Thus, it makes sense to question whether the character understands and believes his or her statement.

In sum, I believe Dickinson sometimes just wanted to articulate a position or a memorable line without endorsing it. She wanted to call something to our attention without having to stand behind it herself. In these cases, she could have used any form she wanted. But I also believe Dickinson sometimes wanted to do more than just articulate a given idea. She wanted to assert it. Either in her own voice or in the voice of a hypothetical person, she wanted to forward it as accurate or true. To succeed at this project, she had to attend to form-content considerations. She had to make sure her form and content aligned with each other. If she had not done so, either she or the "supposed person" in whose voice she was speaking would have fallen prey to a self-contradiction.

THE COGNITIVE VALUE OF POETRY

Granting my picture of Dickinson is accurate, why does it matter? Why is it important to acknowledge she could not have asserted her beliefs in any old way? And why is it worth insisting we can nonetheless paraphrase her works? To answer these questions, it helps to set them against the backdrop of the debate over the value of poetry.

One way to defend poetry is the cognitivist route. According to this approach, poetry is valuable because it can educate and instruct. Good poems matter because they can teach us truths about the world around us and about ourselves. They can get us to recognize and accept insights we would otherwise dismiss or ignore.

Critics of the cognitivist position sometimes concede that poems are able to *give voice* to important truths. But they counter by saying that if we really want to *learn* these truths—if we really want to acquire *knowledge* of them—we are better off consulting other sources. First, poems rarely provide reasons or evidence in support of what they say.[67] Second, as Plato argued in the *Ion*, poets themselves are seldom trained experts concerning the topics they discuss such that we might be justified in accepting the claims they make on their authority. Thus, or so the objection goes, if we really want to be taught about these matters, if we want to acquire knowledge and not merely true beliefs, we ought to look elsewhere. We ought to turn to philosophy or the various sciences, where we find carefully presented arguments and credentialed experts.

It is at this point that the issue of paraphrase comes to the fore. Defenders of poetry argue that we cannot look elsewhere to learn what poems teach us. For it is not possible to say in other words what poems say. The impossibility of paraphrase guarantees that poems

---

67. For discussion, see Noël Carroll, "The Wheel of Virtue."

have unique truths to offer us. It ensures philosophy and the sciences cannot teach us what poetry does.[68]

I do not agree with this view. But I am partial to a moderate version of it. On the one hand, I believe we should accept the possibility of paraphrase. If a poem contains propositional content, then we can articulate it in ordinary prose. There are no propositions only poetry can express.[69] On the other hand, I believe we ought to embrace the idea lying behind the denial of paraphrase. We should accept that poetry has unique cognitive value. Two considerations lend credence to this idea. One is commonly acknowledged. The other gets to the heart of the present chapter.

First, the common point. As noted before, a paraphrase cannot capture all there is to a poem. At best it captures a poem's propositional content. Thus, even a successful paraphrase may miss important things. For instance, it may fail to provide a poem's experiential or emotional meaning. Some of these things are cognitive in nature despite being non-propositional.[70] Consider again "I Felt a Funeral, in My Brain." It gives us knowledge of what it is like to have a mental breakdown. This experiential knowledge is of cognitive value. For it provides us with a benefit that relates to our mental process, functions, and goals. But it is not reducible to a set of propositions. We cannot express the experiential knowledge we gain here in a set of statements about the world. Reading "I Felt a Funeral, in My Brain" may also provide us with a kind of training in how to handle mental trauma. This ability, skill, or know-how is of cognitive value. But, at least on one theory, it too cannot be reduced to a set of propositions.[71]

---

68. Brooks, "The Heresy of Paraphrase," 185; Kivy, *Philosophies of Arts*, 94, 112.
69. For discussion and some possible exceptions, see Camp, "Metaphor and That Certain 'Je Ne Sais Quoi.'"
70. Rowe, "Lamarque and Olsen on Literature and Truth"; Rowe, "Literature, Knowledge, and the Aesthetic Attitude."
71. Ryle, "Knowing How and Knowing That."

So here is one way to defend the unique cognitive value of poetry while allowing for paraphrase. We can say poetry's unique cognitive value lies in the non-propositional but nonetheless cognitive elements of a poem that even a successful paraphrase cannot preserve.

The drawback of this response is that it changes the terms of the debate. Opponents frame their objection to the unique cognitive value of poetry in terms of *propositional* content. They claim it does not convey any distinctive *propositional* truths.[72] Proving poetry has cognitive value of a *non-propositional* sort does not meet this challenge.

In this chapter, I have developed a response that engages opponents on their own terms. I have argued there are some propositions we cannot assert in just any old way. We may be able to *articulate* or *express* them as we see fit. But we cannot *assert* them—we cannot present them as true or represent ourselves as believing them—however we please. We must abide by certain formal or stylistic restrictions on pain of contradiction. In some circumstances, such as those faced by Dickinson, these restrictions require the use of a particular kind of poetic form.

This argument does not establish everything defenders of the no-paraphrase thesis want. It does not prove the unique effability of any particular proposition. It does not prove there are some propositions we can only express in one way. But showing there are some propositions we must assert in a particular kind of poetic form is still an important conclusion. For it secures the indispensable cognitive value of poetry on the narrow terms dictated by its opponents.

72. See, for example, Lamarque and Olsen, *Truth, Fiction, and Literature*; Stolnitz, "On the Cognitive Triviality of Art."

REFERENCES

Allen, Gay Wilson. "Emily Dickinson's Versification." In *The Recognition of Emily Dickinson: Selected Criticism Since 1890*, edited by Caesar R. Blake and Carlton F. Wells, 176–186. Ann Arbor: University of Michigan Press, 1964.

Aumann, Antony. "The Relationship between Aesthetic Value and Cognitive Value." *Journal of Aesthetics and Art Criticism* 72, no. 2 (2014): 117–127.

Bach, Kent, and Robert M. Harnish. *Linguistic Communication and Speech Acts*. Cambridge: Massachusetts Institute of Technology, 1979.

Bache, Christopher M. "Paraphrase and Paraphrasing Metaphors." *Dialectica* 35, no. 3 (1981): 307–326.

Barker, Wendy. "Emily Dickinson and Poetic Strategy." In *The Cambridge Companion to Emily Dickinson*, edited by Wendy Martin, 77–90. Cambridge, UK: Cambridge University Press, 2002.

Beardsley, Monroe C. "Intentions and Interpretations: A Fallacy Revisited." In *The Aesthetic Point of View*, edited by Michael J. Wreen and Donald M. Callen, 188–207. Ithaca: Cornell University Press, 1982.

Black, Max. "How Metaphors Work: A Reply to Donald Davidson." *Critical Inquiry* 6, no. 1 (1979): 131–143.

Black, Max. "Metaphor." *Proceedings of the Aristotelian Society* 55, no. 1 (1954): 273–294.

Black, Max. "More about Metaphor." *Dialectica* 31, no. 3–4 (1977): 431–457.

Blackmur, R. P. "Emily Dickinson: Notes on Prejudice and Fact." In *The Recognition of Emily Dickinson: Selected Criticism Since 1890*, edited by Caesar R. Blake and Carlton F. Wells, 200–223. Ann Arbor: University of Michigan Press, 1964.

Bolinger, Renée Jorgensen. "The Pragmatics of Slurs." *Noûs*, March 1, 2015, 1–24.

Bradley, A. C. *Poetry for Poetry's Sake*. Oxford: Clarendon Press, 1901.

Brooks, Cleanth. "The Heresy of Paraphrase." In *The Well Wrought Urn: Studies in the Structure of Poetry*, 192–214,. Orlando: Harcourt, 1947.

Budick, E. Miller. *Emily Dickinson and the Life of Language: A Study in Symbolic Poetics*. Baton Rouge: Louisiana State University Press, 1985.

Cameron, Sharon. *Choosing Not Choosing*. Chicago: University of Chicago Press, 1992.

Cameron, Sharon. *Lyric Time: Dickinson and the Limits of Genre*. Baltimore: Johns Hopkins University Press, 1981.

Camp, Elisabeth. "Metaphor and That Certain 'Je Ne Sais Quoi.'" *Philosophical Studies* 129, no. 1 (2006): 1–25.

Carroll, Noël. "Art, Intention, and Conversation." In *Intention Interpretation*, edited by Gary Iseminger, 97–131. Philadelphia: Temple University Press, 1992.

Carroll, Noël. "The Wheel of Virtue: Art, Literature, and Moral Knowledge." *Journal of Aesthetics and Art Criticism* 60, no. 1 (2002): 3–26.

Cavell, Stanley. "Aesthetic Problems of Modern Philosophy." In *Must We Mean What We Say? A Book of Essays*, Updated ed., 73–96. Cambridge, UK: Cambridge University Press, 2002.

Culler, Jonathan. *Theory of the Lyric*. Cambridge, MA: Harvard University Press, 2015.

Davidson, Donald. "What Metaphors Mean." *Critical Inquiry* 5, no. 1 (1978): 31–47.

Denman, Kamilla. "Emily Dickinson's Volcanic Punctuation." *The Emily Dickinson Journal* 2, no. 1 (1993): 22–46.

Dickinson, Emily. *The Letters of Emily Dickinson*. 3 vols. Edited by Thomas Herbert Johnson and Theodora Ward. Cambridge, MA: Belknap Press of Harvard University Press, 1958.

Dickinson, Emily, and Helen Vendler. *Dickinson: Selected Poems and Commentaries*. Cambridge, MA: Harvard University Press, 2010.

England, Martha Winburn. "Emily Dickinson and Isaac Watts." In *Hymns UnBidden*, edited by Martha A. Winburn and John Sparrow, 113–147. New York: New York Public Library, 1966.

Erkkila, Betsy. "The Emily Dickinson Wars." In *The Cambridge Companion to Emily Dickinson*, edited by Wendy Martin, 11–29. Cambridge, UK: Cambridge University Press, 2002.

Ford, Karen Jackson. *Gender and the Poetics of Excess: Moments of Brocade*. Jackson: University Press of Mississippi, 2011.

Graham, Gordon. "Aesthetic Cognitivism and the Literary Arts." *Journal of Aesthetic Education* 30, no. 1 (1996): 1–17.

Guyer, Paul. *Values of Beauty: Historical Essays in Aesthetics*. Cambridge, UK: Cambridge University Press, 2005.

Hagenbüchle, Roland. "Precision and Indeterminacy in the Poetry of Emily Dickinson." *Emerson Society Quarterly* 20, no. 1 (1974): 33–56.

Heginbotham, Eleanor Elson. *Reading the Fascicles of Emily Dickinson: Dwelling in Possibilities*. Columbus: Ohio State University Press, 2003.

Higginson, Thomas Wentworth. "Preface to Poems by Emily Dickinson." In *The Recognition of Emily Dickinson: Selected Criticism Since 1890*, edited by Caesar R. Blake and Carlton F. Wells, 10–12. Ann Arbor: University of Michigan Press, 1964.

Hills, David. "Problems of Paraphrase: Bottom's Dream." *Baltic International Yearbook of Cognition, Logic and Communication* 3, no. 1 (2007): 9.

Hulatt, Owen. "The Problem of Modernism and Critical Refusal: Bradley and Lamarque on Form/Content Unity." *Journal of Aesthetics and Art Criticism* 74, no. 1 (2016): 47–59.

Johnson, Thomas Herbert. *Emily Dickinson: An Interpretive Biography*. Cambridge, MA: Belknap Press, 1955.

Kames, [Henry Home] Lord. *Essays on the Principles of Morality and Natural Religion*. London: Hitch & Hawes, 1758.

Kames, Lord [Henry Home]. *Elements of Criticism*. 6th ed. 2 vols. Edited by Peter Jones. Indianapolis, IN: Liberty Fund, 2005.

Kivy, Peter. "Lord Kames and the Sense of Beauty." In *The Seventh Sense: A Study of Francis Hutcheson's Aesthetics and Its Influence on Eighteenth Century Britain*, 260–265. New York: Oxford University Press, 2003.

Kivy, Peter. "Paraphrasing Poetry (for Profit and Pleasure)." *Journal of Aesthetics and Art Criticism* 69, no. 4 (2011): 367–377.

Kivy, Peter. *Philosophies of Arts: An Essay in Differences*. Cambridge, UK: Cambridge University Press, 1997.

Lamarque, Peter. "Poetry and Abstract Thought." *Midwest Studies in Philosophy* 33, no. 1 (September 1, 2009): 37–52.

Lamarque, Peter. "Semantic Finegrainedness and Poetic Value." In *The Philosophy of Poetry*, edited by John Gibson, 18–36. Oxford, UK: Oxford University Press, 2015.

Lamarque, Peter. "The Elusiveness of Poetic Meaning." *Ratio* 22, no. 4 (2009): 398–420.

Lamarque, Peter, and Stein Haugom Olsen. *Truth, Fiction, and Literature: A Philosophical Perspective*. Oxford, UK: Clarendon Press, 1994.

Leighton, Angela. "About About: On Poetry and Paraphrase." *Midwest Studies in Philosophy* 33, no. 1 (2009): 167–176.

Leiter, Sharon. *Critical Companion to Emily Dickinson: A Literary Reference to Her Life and Work*. New York: Infobase Publishing, 2007.

Lepore, Ernie. "Poetry, Medium and Message." *New York Times*, July 31, 2011, sec. The Opinion Pages: The Stone.

Lepore, Ernie. "The Heresy of Paraphrase: When the Medium Really Is the Message." *Midwest Studies in Philosophy* 33, no. 1 (2009): 177–197.

Levinson, Jerrold. "Who's Afraid of a Paraphrase?" *Theoria* 67, no. 1 (April 1, 2001): 7–23.

Lindberg-Seyersted, Brita. *The Voice of the Poet: Aspects of Style in the Poetry of Emily Dickinson*. Cambridge, MA: Harvard University Press, 1968.

Martin, Wendy. *The Cambridge Introduction to Emily Dickinson*. Cambridge, UK: Cambridge University Press, 2007.

McIntosh, James. *Nimble Believing: Dickinson and the Unknown*. Ann Arbor: University of Michigan Press, 2004.

Miles, Susan. "The Irregularities of Emily Dickinson." In *The Recognition of Emily Dickinson: Selected Criticism since 1890*, edited by Caesar R. Blake and Carlton F. Wells, 123–129. Ann Arbor: University of Michigan Press, 1964.

Miller, Cristanne. "Dickinson's Structured Rhythms." In *A Companion to Emily Dickinson*, edited by Martha Nell Smith and Mary Loeffelholz, 391–414. Oxford, UK: Blackwell Publishing, 2007.

Miller, Cristanne. *Emily Dickinson, a Poet's Grammar*. Cambridge, MA: Harvard University Press, 1987.

Monro, Harold. "Emily Dickinson—Overrated." In *The Recognition of Emily Dickinson*, edited by Caesar R. Blake and Carlton F. Wells, 121–122. Ann Arbor: University of Michigan Press, 1964.

Moran, Richard. "Seeing and Believing: Metaphor, Image, and Force." *Critical Inquiry* 16, no. 1 (Autumn 1989): 87–112.

Nathan, Daniel O. "Art, Meaning, and Artist's Meaning." In *Contemporary Debates in Aesthetics and the Philosophy of Art*, edited by Mathew Kieran, 282–293. Malden, MA: Blackwell, 2005.

Nussbaum, Martha C. "Form and Content, Philosophy and Literature." In *Love's Knowledge*, 3–53. Oxford: Oxford University Press, 1990.

Peirce, Charles Sanders. "Judgment and Assertion." In *Collected Papers of Charles Sanders Peirce*, 5: 385–387. Boston, MA: Harvard University Press, 1934.

Porter, David T. *The Art of Emily Dickinson's Early Poetry*. Boston, MA: Harvard University Press, 1966.

Reynolds, David S. "Emily Dickinson and Popular Culture." In *The Cambridge Companion to Emily Dickinson*, edited by Wendy Martin, 167–190. Cambridge, UK: Cambridge University Press, 2002.

Ross, Christine. "Uncommon Measures: Emily Dickinson's Subversive Prosody." *The Emily Dickinson Journal* 10, no. 1 (2001): 70–98.

Rowe, Mark W. "Lamarque and Olsen on Literature and Truth." *Philosophical Quarterly* 47, no. 188 (1997): 322–341.

Rowe, Mark W. "Literature, Knowledge, and the Aesthetic Attitude." *Ratio* 22, no. 4 (2009): 375–397.

Ryle, Gilbert. "Knowing How and Knowing That." In *Collected Papers*, 2: 212–225. New York: Barnes and Nobles, 1971.

Schapiro, Meyer. "On Perfection, Coherence, and Unity of Form and Content." In *Art and Philosophy*, edited by Sidney Hook, 3–15. New York: New York University Press, 1966.

Searle, John. *Speech Acts: An Essay in the Philosophy of Language*. Cambridge: Cambridge University Press, 1969.

Sewall, Richard Benson. *The Life of Emily Dickinson*. 2 vols. Vol. 1. Boston, MA: Harvard University Press, 1994.

Small, Judy Jo. *Positive as Sound: Emily Dickinson's Rhyme*. Athens: University of Georgia Press, 2010.

Spicer, John L. "The Poems of Emily Dickinson." *Boston Public Library Quarterly* 8 (1956): 135–143.

Stolnitz, Jerome. "'Beauty': Some Stages in the History of an Idea." *Journal of the History of Ideas* 22, no. 2 (1961): 185–204.

Stolnitz, Jerome. "On the Cognitive Triviality of Art." *British Journal of Aesthetics* 32, no. 3 (1992): 191–200.

Williams, Bernard. *Truth and Truthfulness: An Essay in Genealogy*. Princeton, NJ: Princeton University Press, 2010.

Williams, Stanley T. "Experiments in Poetry: Emily Dickinson." In *The Recognition of Emily Dickinson: Selected Criticism since 1890*, edited by Caesar R. Blake and Carlton F. Wells, 250–260. Ann Arbor: University of Michigan Press, 1964.

Winters, Yvor. "Primitivism and Decadence: A Study of American Experimental Poetry." In *In Defense of Reason*, 15–150. London: Routledge and Kegan Paul, 1937.

Wolff, Cynthia Griffin. *Emily Dickinson*. New York: Alfred A. Knopf, 1988.

Young, Bruce A. "Snake Bioacoustics: Toward a Richer Understanding of the Behavioral Ecology of Snakes." *Quarterly Review of Biology* 78, no. 3 (2003): 303–325.

Chapter 5

The Uses of Obstruction

DAVID HILLS

That's what they call a metaphor in our country. Don't be afraid of it, sir, it won't bite.

—Valentine from Dickinson to George Gould, February 1850 (L 34)[1]

1.

Dickinson's poems are more accommodating and tentative than their reputation allows. More accommodating, in that they make provision for readers who aren't fully prepared to hear them out. More tentative, in that their characteristic formal devices express a mode of attention that continues to struggle with its object—isn't fully prepared to hear *it* out.

In April of 1862 Dickinson wrote her first letter to Thomas Wentworth Higginson, the one that famously asked, "Are you too deeply occupied to say if my Verse is alive?" (L 260). In December Higginson published in the *Atlantic Monthly* a prose sketch, "The Procession of Flowers," describing some principal New England wildflowers in the

---

1. Dickinson's letters are cited by "L" and their numbers in 1955 (3 vols.). Poems are cited by their numbers in two standard editions: Fr = Franklin, 1999; and J = Johnson, 1960. Texts and composition dates are as given in Franklin.

The Poetry of Emily Dickinson. Elisabeth Camp, Oxford University Press (2021). © Oxford University Press. DOI: 10.1093/oso/9780190651190.003.0006

order of their appearance over the course of a typical year. In January or early February of 1863 Dickinson learned from articles in the *Springfield Republican* that Higginson was in South Carolina commanding a Negro regiment in the Civil War. Her letter to him in February (L 280) reads in part:

> I should have liked to see you, before you became improbable. War feels to me an oblique place - Should there be other Summers, would you perhaps come?
>
> I found you were gone, by accident, as I find Systems are, or Seasons of the year, and obtain no cause - but suppose it a treason of Progress - that dissolves as it goes. Carlo [my dog] still remained - and I told him -
>
> Best Gains - must have the Losses' Test
> To constitute them - Gains -
>
> My Shaggy Ally assented . . .
> I trust you may pass the limit of War, and though not reared to prayer - when service is had in Church, for Our Arms, I include yourself . . .
> But I fear I detain you -
> Should you, before this reaches you, experience immortality, who will inform me of the Exchange? Could you, with honor, avoid Death, I entreat you - Sir - it would bereave
>
> > Your Gnome -
> I trust the "Procession of Flowers" was not a premonition.

This shows concern for Higginson's fate but no concern at all for the fate of the cause for which he was risking his life. Imagine receiving such a letter yourself and sitting down to compose a reply. You fear you detain me—from what exactly? If you "trust" my writing about flowers wasn't a premonition of my death, why go out of your way to suggest that's just what it was? You have the perversity to ask *me* whose job it is to inform you of *my death—if I'm already dead?* I might as well be, apparently. You won't forgive my seeming to put slavery and its abolition ahead of your verse and its life, so you write me into an impossible corner on purpose.

Yet there is poetry of a high order in the surmise about progress at the letter's core. Many are prepared to think or say that we don't know what we've got till it's gone. But that isn't the half of it. We don't *have* what we've got till it's gone, until its loss *constitutes* it as a significant acquisition, a Gain, in retrospect. If progress didn't dissolve as it went, it wouldn't be progress.

Such a letter shouldn't be missed. It is a privilege to read it. But I'm grateful it wasn't addressed to me. It deprives its addressee of ground to stand on while taking it in and composing a fit response— deprives him of standing, period. David Bromwich notes that the letters of Keats and Dickinson "are beautiful and fraught, always special, often at the stretch, and they pass the full test of character with a vengeance: they would burn a hole in any other prose you set beside them."[2] But the cases are very different. Keats's letters don't threaten to burn a hole in their recipient. They don't actively preclude the response in kind they urgently solicit. Dickinson's do.

Condescension plays a role in all this. Uncomfortable as she may have been in her various inherited identities, Dickinson renounced none of them. She remained enough of a patrician to marvel at the involuntary animal openness of her own servants (L 337). She remained enough of a Calvinist and enough of a Whig to patronize the assorted Unitarians, Transcendentalists, agnostics, Abolitionists, and social reformers she relied on for literary inspiration and spiritual companionship.

But something else is at work as well. Dickinson seemed constitutionally unable to write or speak or think except in terms that required

2. Bromwich, *Skeptical Music: Essays on Modern Poetry*, 56.

active interpretation. To contend with her, interlocutors always had to contend with her distinctive ways of putting things. This wore them out, understandably:

> The young Dickinson was so volatile, so volcanic in her intuitions that she could clear a room. Mental and emotional acuity on that level is frightening because people have no way of explaining its source. It requires no nurturing. It expands not only without the intervention of other people but against the will of the person who possesses it—or is possessed by it. It simply happens. Not many people want to have tea with the Delphic oracle, however mesmerizing her speech . . .
>
> Dickinson's reclusiveness was not a way of protecting herself from the world but a way of protecting the world from herself. . . . The language of poetry was not fit for all occasions, since even the slightest release of it into the real world could be explosive.[3]

Precisely. Yet this might tempt us to neglect important differences between the poetry in Dickinson's conversation and correspondence and the poetry in her poems—a mistake nobody dreams of making in the case of Keats! To be sure, Dickinson insisted on the explosiveness of all poetry, her own included:

> If I read a book and it makes my whole body so cold no fire ever can warm me, that is poetry. If I feel physically as if the top of my head were taken off, I know that is poetry. These are the only way I know it. Is there any other way?[4]

---

3. Longenbach, *The Virtues of Poetry*, 59.
4. In conversation with Higginson, 1870. See his "Emily Dickinson's Letters," *Atlantic Monthly* 68 (1891): 444–456. Cited in Sewall, *The Life of Emily Dickinson*, 566.

Dickinson's poems traffic in explosive thoughts about explosive themes: pain, violence, ecstasy, erotic obsession, the loss through death of loved ones, the death-in-life of chronic estrangement. But they manage to be less volatile, less volcanic, friendlier to the needs and appetites and limitations of readers or listeners, than Dickinson's conversation and correspondence. Coming to terms with them is an arduous and open-ended task, but it isn't tea with the Delphic oracle. The poems are ready to meet readers halfway, and equipped to do so, in ways I would like to understand.

Imitation may be the sincerest form of flattery but it's a risky form of description, risky for the dignity of the describer and the integrity of the thing described. Yet something about the sounds and shapes of Dickinson's verse inspires imitation from otherwise cool-headed, otherwise cautious describers.

In his brief guide to the structures of English verse, *Rhyme's Reason,* John Hollander observes:

> The ballad stanza in a hymn
>> Waits on the music's pleasure,
> And hymnals (hardly out of whim)
>> Call it the "common measure."
>
> (The attic heart's - theology
> Reformed - this hymnal scheme
> In Emily Dickinson's - Amherst - house
> And slanted - away - the rhyme.)[5]

Or as he puts it more prosaically elsewhere:

> Using a basis of the so-called "common meter" of hymnody—the accentual version in 4-beat and 3-beat

---

5. Hollander, *Rhyme's Reason: A Guide to English Verse,* 16–17.

alternating lines of the tetrameter-trimeter *abcb* rhyming quatrain often called "ballad stanza"—[Dickinson] derived an intense, chromatic, often deliberately soured, solo hymnody of her own.[6]

Dickinson's use of meter, rhyme, and stanza is more varied and deliberate than some of her admirers realize, yet the combination of hymn scheme and slant rhyme is characteristic; she resorts to it regularly as a kind of default.

Quoting from the "mock heroic" "Bloom - is Result" (Fr 1038, J 1058; 1865):

> To pack the Bud - oppose the Worm -
> Obtain its right of Dew -
> Adjust the Heat - Elude the Wind -
> Escape the prowling Bee -

Helen Vendler ventures as an imitative paraphrase:

> To pack the Line - oppose Cliché -
> Obtain its right of Song -
> Adjust the Pace - Elude the Coarse -
> Escape the Lurking Wrong - [7]

Dickinson's verse is terse, telegraphic even. It derives its singing and speaking voices from adjustments in pace—subtle speedings up and slowings down—rather than from the assonance and alliteration we find in Keats and Stevens or the intricate imitations of spontaneous speech we find in Browning and Frost. It achieves novelties of

6. Hollander, *Vision and Resonance: Two Senses of Poetic Form*, 233.
7. Vendler, *Dickinson: Selected Poems and Commentaries*, 8.

thought and feeling by aiming straight at something stale, familiar, manifestly wrong or at least, manifestly thin—and veering away at the last possible moment.

Which brings me to Dickinson's notorious dashes or hyphens, her "hesitation marks." Susan Howe comments on them, deploying her own periods as if they were Dickinsonian dashes:

> A "sheltered" woman audaciously invented a new grammar grounded in humility and hesitation, HESITATE from the Latin, meaning to stick. Stammer. To hold back from doubt, have difficulty speaking. . . . Dashes drew liberty of interruption inside the structure of each poem. Hush of hesitation for breath and for breathing.[8]

Effective as these imitations may be for their special pedagogical purposes, they put Dickinsonian devices to utterly un-Dickinsonian use. Their authors know from the start precisely what they mean to say *about* the devices *with* the devices, and do so with a minimum of fuss. In Dickinson's own hands the devices constitute a self-questioning, self-correcting, self-censoring *mode of attention*: hesitant, probing, swift and slow, bold and discreet, conventional and unconventional by turns, inventing as it goes the specific formal and metrical constraints it proceeds to respect. The imitators' use of the devices is all exposition, her own use is all exploration. The irregular short lines and loose, improvised forms of Emerson's poems made a lasting impression upon her—as did his habit of interrupting himself to enriching self-corrective effect. Compare "I taste a liquor never brewed" (Fr 207, J 214; 1861) with Emerson's "Bacchus."

8. Howe, *My Emily Dickinson*, 21–22.

We can begin to sense how Dickinson means to accommodate readers and cope with her own tentativeness when we turn from her use of scheme to her use of trope. Metaphors and related figures of speech are routinely prized for affording us a cognitive grip we'd otherwise lack on objects we're eager to understand. Two important poems by Dickinson stand this familiar conception on its head. In them she explicitly advises herself about how to write, hence implicitly advises us about how to read her. So I'll call them *advisories*. According to them,

(1) Human frailty is such that certain important truths about important objects must be insinuated or intimated rather than bluntly and directly stated if we are to take them in and take them to heart. There needn't be anything ineffable about these truths. Blunt direct statement of them may be entirely possible. But it would be futile, in that we wouldn't be able to confirm and absorb what we'd been bluntly, directly told.

(2) Our view of an important object can often be improved— rendered more cognitively fruitful—if it is obstructed, obscured, or softened by the insertion between us and it of a second object, through which and by means of which we scrutinize it. Figurative language is one way to provide such enabling obstructions.

The advisories call on figurative language to obstruct, obscure, and soften our view of objects that are entirely too available already, objects whose access to us must be impeded if the truth about them is to be squarely faced and stably absorbed. They offer distinct but compatible proposals as to *how* obstructing our view of an important object can improve our view of it. Such calls come as a surprise, given

Dickinson's well-earned reputation for vehemence, bluntness, and imagistic violence.

2.

Our first advisory comes from very early in Dickinson's career:

> The thought beneath so slight a film -
> Is more distinctly seen -
> As laces just reveal the surge -
> Or Mists - the Apennine
>
> (Fr 210, J 203; 1861)

The Apennines are a mountain range in Northern Italy. Dickinson's hymnal scheme is in evidence here; one could easily sing this to the tune of "O God Our Help in Ages Past. And the slant rhyme of "seen" and "Apennine" calls attention to the poem's core puzzle: how mists serve to *reveal* mountains they *enshroud* and *occlude*.

The diction in the third line may seem too terse for its own good. What kind of laces, what kind of surge? There are laces on shoes, laces on doilies on the backs of chairs, etc. And almost any abrupt movement of fluid or abrupt onset of feeling—indeed, almost anything abrupt—can count as a surge. Perhaps we should start with the misty mountains and work back.

Here are two paintings by Caspar David Friedrich, from closely related points of view, of a single vista in the Giant Mountains, the Riesengebirge. The first is a watercolor done in full midday sunlight:

Figure 5.1 Caspar David Friedrich, *Landscape in the Riesengebirge* (date unknown), watercolor and pencil. Oskar Reinhart Foundation, Winterthur.

The second is an oil, depicting the mountains as the mists of morning are beginning to burn off:

Figure 5.2 Caspar David Friedrich, *Giant Mountains Landscape with Rising Fog* (1819–20), oil on canvas. Neue Pinakothek, Munich.

The second, obstructed view may strike some of us as better, topographically more informative, than the unobstructed one, thanks in part to the way mist collects in valleys and passes and other low spots, in part to the way successively more distant peaks are obscured by successively thicker layers of haze. There are trade-offs, to be sure: certain contours of the hillsides and details of vegetation are visible in the first view but invisible in the second. But a newcomer trying to get her bearings in the terrain would be happy to make such tradeoffs.

All of which suggests two possible ways to take "As *laces* just reveal the *surge*." Spectators in a room with an open window may *see* a brisk wind they are in no position to *feel* if the window's lace curtains are driven in dancing zigzags by the wind's successive gusts or surges. Spectators atop a seaside cliff might perceive the moving crests and troughs and swells— surges—of the dark water at the foot of the cliff, thanks only to laces of foam or froth that ride atop them, carried along by them, occluding any direct view of them. We'll be hard pressed to choose between these readings if both occur to us, and hard pressed to persuade ourselves there isn't a more appropriate reading lurking in the wings.[9]

A second poem about veiling may qualify and enrich our application of this one:

Our lives are Swiss -
So still - so Cool -
Till some odd afternoon
The Alps neglect their Curtains
And we look farther on!

9. Dickinson was notoriously indifferent to orthodox spelling, so *surge* could be an unorthodox spelling of *serge*. Serge is silk or wool or cotton that's twilled, woven so as to leave visible parallel diagonal ridges—a fabric built for durability rather than looks. So perhaps we are to imagine a serge dress covered in part with openwork lace trim, built for looks rather than durability. For as long as it lasts, the delicacy of the lace would set off and bring out the ruggedness of the underlying garment visible through it and around it. I owe this suggestion to Paul Woodruff.

Italy stands the other side!
While like a guard between -
The solemn Alps -
The siren Alps
Forever intervene!

(Fr 129, J 80; 1859)

Dickinson's "Switzerland" is a lot like Broadway's Brigadoon: a village surrounded by mists so thick, the inhabitants forget the mountain barrier surrounding it on every side—forget their village has sur- roundings at all—until one day the mountains get forgetful and fail to draw their curtains. When that day comes, the inhabitants "look farther on," past the mountains they see for the first time toward an Italy they still can't see at all. The sudden imaginative spotting of a still invisible Italy beyond the newly visible Alps is signaled by an italicized anapestic substitution, "*Italy* stands." The Alps are "solemn" Alps, since they prohibit access to what lies on the other side, and "siren" Alps, since they would lure inhabitants to their doom in efforts to defy that prohibition. So this is a poem about Eden, with Alps fill- ing in for the Angel with the Fiery sword.—How can the sight of the Alps afford an idea of *Italy* to creatures who previously lacked any idea *even of the Alps?*—By confronting them with a manifest barrier.

Montaigne says in "On Presumption":[10]

It is commonly held that good sense is the gift which Nature has most fairly shared among us, since there is nobody who is not satisfied with what Nature has allotted him. And is that not rea- sonable? Anyone who would peer beyond it would be peering beyond what his sight can reach.

10. Montaigne, *The Complete Essays*, 746.

Montaigne argues or pretends to argue that since none of us can peer beyond what her own sight can reach, each of us is or reasonably can be satisfied with the sightedness she already has: grounds for dissatisfaction are necessarily lacking. The distribution of sense is necessarily fair, whether or not it is equitable, whether or not all get equal shares. (How would we know whether our shares are equal in any case? And if we can't know, why should we care?)

"Our lives are Swiss" argues to the contrary that each of us can and does "look further on," peering with a mixture of imagination and longing into matters her sense of sight, such as it is, *can't* reach to any satisfying extent. And when we do, each of us can and does find herself wanting when it comes to good sense. Here imagination and longing function cognitively, teaching us something sense can't teach us about sense's standing limitations. As long as we can reasonably imagine and yearn for more than sense can deliver, grounds for dissatisfaction with it are necessarily present. Our shares of it will seem puny and unfair, no matter how evenly it's distributed.

What "The thought beneath so slight a film" adds is a suggestion that if imagination and longing function to *criticize* sense's reach, they also function to *extend* it—in special ways in special cases. When we see not *despite* but *by means of* obstructions, it's because imagination and longing come to participate in the work of sense. It is only when a second object is interposed between us and our main object of attention and concern, spoiling or degrading our view of some of its features, that others of its features become visible for the first time.

3.

There are non-metaphorical ways to do this trick. A poem might challenge us to spot a familiar thing or kind of thing behind a scrim woven from its characteristic features or effects or accompaniments.

In that case the operative figure of speech is metonymy. Dickinson wrote numerous riddle poems that operate along such lines.

> A Route of Evanescence,
> With a revolving Wheel -
> A Resonance of Emerald
> A rush of Cochineal -
> And every Blossom on the Bush
> Adjusts it's tumbled Head -
> The Mail from Tunis - probably,
> An easy Morning's Ride -

(Fr 1489, J 1463; 1879)

The answer to the riddle this time is "Hummingbird." Dickinson mounts her Hummingbird on a spinning Wheel, thereby accounting for the roughly circular blur of its wings and its unbirdlike power to back up or hold still in midair. As for "The Mail from Tunis": in Shakespeare's *Tempest* Prospero's fellow Neapolitans shipwreck on his isle while returning from the wedding of Alonso's daughter Claribel to the King of Tunis, an African city so appallingly far from Naples, father and daughter can have "no note" from each other in the future "unless the sun were post" (*The Tempest* 2.1). Our bird is credited with a sunlike power to conquer distance.

A second riddle poem brings in personification—hence metaphor of a sort, if we suppose that to personify a thing is to metaphorically liken it to some particular sort of person:

> A Visitor in Marl -
> Who influences Flowers -
> Till they are orderly as Busts -
> And Elegant - As Glass -

Who visits in the Night -
And just before the Sun -
Concludes his glistening interview -
Caresses - and is gone -

But whom his fingers touched -
And where his feet have run -
And whatsoever mouth he kissed -
Is as it had not been -

(Fr 558, J 391; 1863)

This time the answer to the riddle is "Frost." Marl, I take it, is fabric woven from variegated yarn; it can exhibit a convincingly frostlike shimmer. Here the decisive clues to the riddle come in the second stanza. The first stanza dwells on Frost's power to transfigure ordinary objects to entrancing effect. The coercive undertone in "orderly as Busts" is audible only in retrospect. Only in the third stanza, when Frost mutates from a tidying "influence" into a departing lover, is its power to transfigure linked to its power to blight and destroy. Even there, its destructive power is touched on in the lightest and most deniable way possible. The final line, "Is as it had not been," is three ways ambiguous. It could mean *Is as it hadn't been before*, reiterating Frost's already admitted, already fascinating power to transfigure. It could mean *Is changed irrevocably*, issuing a warning but leaving us free to prefer the transfigured things to their originals if we wish. Or it could mean *Is as if it had never been at all*, making Frost's kiss the kiss of death. The poem is only as dark as a given reader lets it get—such is the power and function of euphemism in this corner of Dickinson's work.

My final example is firmly and emphatically metaphorical—and firmly and emphatically dark. It takes a close unflinching look at a human death—a sudden, convulsive, waking death—by likening it to the abrupt seizing up of a piece of clockwork.

A Clock stopped -
Not the Mantel's -
Geneva's farthest skill
Cant put the puppet bowing -
That just now dangled still -

An awe came on the Trinket!
The Figures hunched - with pain -
Then quivered out of Decimals -
Into Degreeless noon -

It will not stir for Doctor's -
This Pendulum of snow -
The Shopman importunes it -
While cool - concernless no -

Nods from the Gilded pointers -
Nods from the Seconds slim -
Decades of Arrogance between
The Dial life -
And Him -

(Fr 259, J 287; 1861)

The presence of this metaphor is signaled four times over. There's the second stanza's attribution of "awe" and "pain" to what had previously just been a Clock. There's the second stanza's pairing of a Shopman importuning a Clock with a Doctor importuning his patient. There's all that talk about Snow and coolness and Degreelessness: we creatures get cold as we die and stiffen, but a Clock gets no colder when it freezes up. And there's the reference in the fourth stanza to a "Dial life" separated from its Creator by "Decades of Arrogance": humans have lifespans measurable in Decades.

Most of the poem's lines have three beats each. But it opens and closes abruptly in pairs of two-beat lines, the very first line and the very last being strongly spondaic. The other conspicuous metrical incident is a thumpingly dactylic enactment of a pair of nods:

Nods from the Gilded pointers -
Nods from the Seconds slim -

The poem begins with a stopped clock and ends with a Divine Watchmaker. It alludes to William Paley's presentation of the Argument from Design, something Dickinson would have encountered as a schoolgirl:

"Suppose I had found a watch upon the ground." Just as the existence of a watch indicates the existence of a watchmaker, so all ordered processes around us indicate the informing presence of a Master Craftsman.[11]

As worked out here, the allusion carries a blasphemous Humean hint that if we can argue from purposive order in natural things to intelligently purposeful activity on the part of an agent responsible for that order, we can likewise argue from manifest defects in workmanship to culpable limitations in the Workman responsible. And susceptibility to sudden and irreversible seizing up is a defect in workmanship if anything is.

I speak of a *close* look at death, not a *good* look, since the decisive essentials of what goes on as a person dies can't be witnessed by onlookers, no matter how hard they look. (That's Dickinson's view at any rate. See "This World is not conclusion" [Fr 373, J 501; 1862] and L 332). Even a close look at death won't easy to come by. We sometimes actively avoid or inadvertently miss the deaths of those closest

11. Wolff, *Emily Dickinson*, 191.

to us, those whose deaths could mean the most to us. And when we do witness death face to face, an anxious and bewildered concern for the one dying may have us too busy watching ourselves, too busy monitoring our own reactions, to watch death happen as it happens. We watch it closely only in retrospect, collecting and reviewing our impressions of it after the fact. Metaphor is one way to gather scattered retrospective impressions into a critical mass.

The primary subject, the death, swims into view slowly and reluctantly. Before we encounter any literal mention of it, we encounter a puppet that first "bows," then "dangles still"—as if it had been hanged and not merely hung up. How does this puppet relate to the stopped Clock with which we began? That depends on what we make later on of "Figures" that first "hunch" (with pain) then "quiver" (with awe)— which depends in turn on the nature we attribute to the Clock.

Perhaps the Figures are numerals on the face of a conventional pendulum clock, a Grandfather clock.[12] It's hard to see how they could "hunch," then "quiver," except as the result of an accumulation and subsequent release of tension in the whole body of the clock. In that case the poem likens the clock and its seizing up to a puppet and its hanging up by a puppeteer, in preparation for a subsequent likening of that hanging up to a human death. The Figures "quiver out of Decimals" in that they abandon their usual time-telling mission.

Perhaps we are dealing with a smaller and fancier wall clock, along the lines of the Chalet clocks and Black Forest clocks that remain in production to this day.[13] Such a clock would have a short pendulum and weights on chains hanging down below its body. Little carved doll people (Figures) would emerge from its insides to bow or curtsey to us every hour, on the hour. The puppet would literally be part of the clockwork, "hunched" to begin its bow or curtsey when the

---

12. Vendler, *Dickinson: Selected Poems and Commentaries*, 89 ff.
13. Anderson, *Emily Dickinson's Poetry: Stairway of Surprise*, 266.

clock as a whole seizes up, then "quivering" when the shock of this seizure gives everything in the clock a good hard shake. The end of the clock's capacity to keep time and the end of the puppet's servile gesticulations would be simultaneous effects of a common cause.

Or perhaps we are to stuff clockwork into a doll rather than the other way round: perhaps we are dealing with a one of the intricate clockwork automata Geneva watchmakers turned out for advertising purposes back in the eighteenth century. A team headed by Pierre Jaquet-Droz constructed several such showpieces. The most astonishing, *The Writer*, is a 6,000-piece mechanical boy, programmed with interchangeable cams to scrawl a desired message on paper using a quill he dips in an inkpot.[14] Dickinson wouldn't have seen such contraptions, but she could certainly read about them. In that case puppet and clock would be one and the same; the decommissioning (hanging up) of the puppet would simply be the seizing up of the clockwork. (I say *would be*, since *The Writer* remains in good working order to this day in a museum in Neuchâtel.) Such contraptions move so regularly that they *keep* time: we could measure its passage by watching their movements if we saw fit.

Each way of elaborating Dickinson's image has its own appeal and its own limitations. I don't think we can choose among them, and I don't think we're called on to do so. Dickinson offers a poetical *sketch* in which a single contour gets rendered by a tangle of three distinct lines, none of which could replace the tangle to which it belongs. The imagined mechanical breakdown that brings death *into* focus remains itself *out of* focus, the better to be seen *through*.

This would be hard to understand if metaphor always set us peering at a primary subject (or tenor) through a scrim of specific *resemblances to* or *analogies with* its secondary subject (or vehicle). If it did, our view of the secondary subject would need to be at least as clear as the view of the primary

---

14. See Riskin, *The Restless Clock: A History of the Centuries-Long Argument over What Makes Living Things Tick*, 128–132.

subject it made possible. The matter becomes less mysterious if we suppose that metaphor arranges or stages a performance on the part of the primary subject in which it assumes the role or plays the part of the secondary subject. The view-enhancing film over the primary subject (a death) is provided by efforts to recognize the secondary subject (the stopping of a clock) in the performance the primary subject turns in when retrospectively cast in this role. We see a death (vividly) by trying to discern *in* it (however dimly and sketchily) the enacted breakdown of some kind of timepiece.

What we observe when we do so is a (dutiful) bow, interrupted by a (pained) hunch, breaking into a quiver (of awe or astonishment), succeeded by a nod (of refusal) . . . that at last gives way to a permanent dangling stillness. The death here is sudden and hard, in contrast to the slow and easy death figured in "After great pain a formal feeling comes":

As Freezing persons, recollect the Snow -
First - Chill - then Stupor - then the letting go -

(Fr 372, J 341; 1862)

Here a pained hunch takes the place of "Chill," a shocked and quivering apprehensiveness (awe) takes the place of "Stupor," and an active refusal of importunings from attending experts takes the place of "letting go." The two sequences are powerfully different: only in "A Clock stopped" is death the culmination of a painful and conscious ordeal that leaves onlookers indignant, wondering why death ever needs to be like this. (They are surprisingly alike in another respect. While slow death involves a passive acquiescence in what's coming, "letting go," abrupt and violent death involves the active repudiation of what's gone before, "cool concernless no." Put the two stories together and it seems to follow that nobody ever dies unwillingly.)

A hard and sudden death from seizing up suggests recalcitrance or intractability on the part of the one who dies; a slow and easy death from running down doesn't. So what looks from one point of view like punishment of the designed by the designer, looks from another like a rebellion against the designer by the designed, a willed deafness to the designer's importunings, in which case death is an abrupt refusal to go on as before.

The poem is indignant but unclear about the grounds of its indignation. Is it that we have to die at all? That some of us get to drift off in our sleep while others have the life shaken out of us with painful and alarming violence? Or that creatures destined for eternity must keep time or do time or serve time *first*—that before being taken up into eternity, we must live earthly lives?

4.

It seems to me that with

> A Clock stopped -
> Not the Mantel's -

we sense we are dealing with death before we know the stopped clock is *a metaphor for* death. The first two lines read like a euphemistic death announcement designed to go over the heads of any children who might overhear it. Might there be metaphors that owe their lasting effectiveness as metaphors to their temporary effectiveness as euphemisms?

The question brings me to the other advisory poem I want to consider. It offers a different model of how obstructing a view might serve to improve it:

> Tell all the truth but tell it slant -
> Success in Circuit lies

Too bright for our infirm Delight
The Truth's superb surprise

As Lightning to the Children eased
With explanation kind
The Truth must dazzle gradually
Or every man be blind -

(Fr 1263, J 1129; 1872)[15]

"Circuit" is Dickinsonian shorthand or telegraphese for circuitous-ness, roundaboutness, indirection. The truth we are urged to tell is wild, inchoate, vivid, challenging—able to inspire respect and delight, yet hard to handle epistemically, emotionally, and practically. We'll be blind to such truth or flinch away from it if it rushes in on us all at once. Yet we accommodate it successfully if it dawns on us, breaks in on us, a bit at a time.

Our eyes are dazzled and blinded by the full light of day if we are exposed to it abruptly after a long stay in the dark. Yet we can take it in eventually if we step out into it gradually, exposing ourselves to it a bit at a time. Each level of illumination we take in prepares us to cope with a somewhat higher level, until we are ready to cope with the full light of day. It's a matter of giving our pupils—the pupils of our eyes, that is—sufficient time to adjust and sufficient incentive to do so.

Human children would be unwilling or unable to absorb the whole truth about lightning, presented in an unvarnished literal account of lightning's nature and power and danger. They'd find such an account unintelligible, frightening, patronizing—or all three at once. Yet they can *come* to absorb and appreciate the whole truth about lightning if we arrange for it to dawn on them a bit at a time as

---

15. "Dazzle gradually" replaces "dazzle *moderately*" in an earlier version—a momentous change. See Vendler, *Dickinson: Selected Poems and Commentaries*, 432.

they take in, reinterpret, and eventually outgrow a beginner-friendly myth about lightning. The first bit of truth they recover prepares them intellectually and emotionally for the next bit, until at last they recover and absorb all of it.

Dickinson doesn't view efforts to stretch out the reception of truth as objectionably dishonest. She doesn't think they spoil one of the most precious things about Truth: its "superb surprise." She thinks they make appropriate allowance for "our infirm Delight," something feeble or unhealthy in our capacity to take pleasure where pleasure is called for. Each of these points is or should be controversial.

"Tell it slant" is a figure of speech in its own right, *anthimeria*, where a word or phrase belonging by established usage or internal syntax to one part of speech gets used and interpreted as if it belonged to some other part of speech entirely. ("The cattle nooned in the shade of the trees": here "noon" is a noun used and interpreted as a verb. The cattle took shelter from the midday sun in the shade of the trees.) In this case "slant" is a verb used to successful adverbial effect: we are to tell the truth circuitously—in a roundabout, delay-inducing manner.[16] How does this work? How does "slant" come to mean any such thing in this particular context? There are at least three possibilities here:

(1) a pole or board or plank is slanted or aslant when it is oblique, at an angle, neither fully vertical nor fully horizontal in orientation; and language is regularly said to be oblique when it is

---

16. The point is a delicate one. The word "slant" has routine nominal and adjectival uses as well as verbal uses. It even has an established old-fashioned adverbial use, on which to do something slant is to do it slantingly or slopingly, in a slanting or sloping direction or manner. Light can fall slant. Scissors can cut slant. One could hold something slant if one held it at an angle to its usual orientation. But an action must involve spatial movement or orientation to admit of this kind of adverbial modification, and telling doesn't.

    less than direct. So telling it slant could be a matter of telling it indirectly.

(2)   to tell something straight is to be candid or forthright about it; to be straight with one's audience is to be candid or forthright with it; in its more geometric uses "straight" regularly serves as an opposite of "oblique" or "slanted" or "aslant." So telling it slant could be a matter of telling it in a way that's less than candid or forthright.

(3)   to drink (or otherwise take), to serve (or otherwise give) something straight (or straight up) is to drink it (or take it), serve it (or give it), neat or undiluted. And again, in its more geometric uses "straight" stands opposed to "oblique" or "slanted" or "aslant." So telling it slant could be a matter of telling it in a way that dilutes it so as to diffuse or delay its impact.

Each of these etymologies puts its own spin to "telling it slant." The poem provides no basis for favoring one of them over the others.

    To think of metaphorical likening this way is to regard fuller and fuller paraphrases of a metaphor as successive stages in a process of demythologizing our first take on its primary subject. Successful reception of part of the truth prepares us for the successful reception of more of it. Dickinson declares that poetry must come as a shock to the reader's system, but a cushioned blow is still a blow.

    What sort of explanation of lightning might Dickinson offer the neighborhood children out of kindness? Vague memories of the game of ninepins in "Rip van Winkle" had me speculating about celestial bowling alleys, until I came across this:

> The Lightning is a yellow Fork
> From Tables in the Sky
> By inadvertent fingers dropt
> The awful Cutlery

Of mansions never quite disclosed
And never quite concealed
The Apparatus of the Dark
To ignorance revealed -

(Fr 1140, J 1173; 1867)

Think of a branching bolt of lightning as an immense golden fork falling from the sky. It might spear us, wounding or killing us, if we were unlucky enough to be standing under it when it falls. (A timely warning about lightning's real dangers.) But think of this fork as part of a place setting in some grand celestial banquet hall. Then it is cutlery, but it isn't weaponry—it's a civilized implement, not a savage one. It isn't out to get us but is inadvertently dropped into our world from the higher, grander world where it belongs. That much less to be afraid of. But that much less room for resentment if someone near and dear should one day fall victim to lightning—and that much less room to regard the powers above as scrupulously attentive to the needs and vulnerabilities of their downstairs neighbors. Accidents will happen. What really needs explaining—or if we can't explain it, what really needs to be noticed—isn't Lightning as such but the grand and inscrutable residence in which its glorious appearance and formidable power are fully at home.

As for "The Apparatus of the Dark," Dickinson is equally at home with the conjecture that God is too bright for our infirm delight and the contrary-sounding conjecture that he is too dark for our infirm understanding. For the first she could cite Milton's Nativity Ode on the "light insufferable" Christ set aside for our sake in becoming human. For the second she could cite the end of Henry Vaughn's "The Night":

> But living where the sun
> Doth all things wake, and where all mix and tire

Themselves and others, I consent and run
    To every mire,
And by this world's ill-guiding light,
Err more than I can do by night.

    There is in God, some say,
A deep but dazzling darkness, as men here
Say it is late and dusky, because they
    See not all clear.
O for that night! where I in Him
Might live invisible and dim!

Numbering God among the forces of darkness needn't deprive him of his power to dazzle. As Plato says in the *Republic*, "Anyone with any sense . . . would remember that eyes may be confused in two ways, and from two causes: when they change from the light into the darkness, or from the darkness into the light" (Plato, 2004, 7, 517e-518a).

5.

Is there a general poetic practice of which "Tell all the truth but tell it slant" is the theory? Are there poems that yield increasingly challenging meanings on successive passes through their language and imagery, each pass preparing us for the next?

Anthony Hecht offers a reading of "The Soul selects her own Society" that adheres to this model pretty convincingly.

The Soul selects her own Society -
Then - shuts the Door -
To her divine Majority -
Present no more -

Unmoved - she notes the Chariots - pausing -
At her low Gate -
Unmoved - an Emperor be kneeling -
Opon her Mat -

I've known her - from an ample nation -
Choose One -
Then - close the Valves of her attention -
Like Stone -

(Fr 409, J 303; 1862)

"Choose One - " / "Like Stone": two short spondaic lines linked by a slant rhyme. The lengthening of the vowel provides a note of finality and a sense of closure. And the rhyme itself suggests we look for something stony or stone-like—something unforgiving, inflexible, or hard—about the soul's selection process.

The proud reclusiveness readers of Dickinson regularly thrill to is certainly there, yet it doesn't get the last word:

The poem is not usually conceived of as a riddle, but rather as a description of those instinctive preferences and choices, those defiantly nonrational elections and allegiances, like love, that we all make, without regard to personal advantage, to rank, or to estate. . . . The mixed metaphor of the last two lines . . . could be rather comfortably resolved if we substituted "heart" for "soul," since hearts can be "stony" and they have valves.

But I suggest that the power of the poem derives from a suppressed riddle, an unstated but implied parallel. As the soul is to its society (absolute, arbitrary, ruthless), so is God in his election and salvation of souls. Moreover, it seems to me that the second stanza not improbably suggests the adoration of the Magi, though I have no care to press that point. Still, the ominous quality of the final words is considerably amplified when the ultimate mystery of election is taken into account. We play at being God; it is characteristically human of us to do so.[17]

This final conclusion about us—that in selecting our own society we arrogantly play at being God—is a blow that must be delayed and softened if we are to fully absorb it. Although Hecht doesn't say so explicitly, the ominousness of the poem's final words derives from a reinterpretation of the mixed metaphor they contain. Reading "Valves," we think first and foremost of the flaps the heart opens and closes to take in and let go of blood, flaps which won't work properly if they harden and turn stony. The organ of feeling also known as the heart is likewise in the business of taking in and letting go, likewise in danger of becoming too hard. But we soon reflect that the Valves of *God's* attention are real stones sealing up real tombs. Opening one's heart to let a select few in is dismayingly analogous to opening a tomb to let a select few out. Pascal said the heart has its reasons of which reason knows nothing. The poem begins in solidarity with Pascal. But if Hecht is right, that solidarity seeps away as we continue to read and reflect.

We can think of Hecht's reading as proceeding through three stages or phases:

First comes a *Reclusive* phase, during which the Soul proudly insists on her autonomy in choosing the handful of companions who henceforth constitute her Society. (All of us make such fateful and unaccountable choices, and most of us make them "without regard to personal advantage, to rank, or to estate"—a fact which undermines the pride we are inclined to take in making them as we do.)

Next comes a *Calvinist* phase, during which the analogy between the mystery of the Soul's choices about whom to select

17. Hecht, "The Riddles of Emily Dickinson," 108–109.

and the mystery of God's choices about whom to save is pressed home. Reference to withdrawal from "her *divine* Majority" in the first stanza and the buried allusion to the Magi in the second help this along.

A bewildered *Final* phase begins with shock at the presumptu-ousness of likening our own choice of companions to God's choice of his elect. It goes on to reflect that what makes these choices alike is their "absolute, arbitrary, ruthless" character. But a choice that is absolute, arbitrary, and ruthless in the eyes of its maker is nothing for that maker to take pride in—hardly a real choice in the first place. It's no surprise when God's choices fail to make sense to us. But when our own choices fail to do so, it's time to wonder whether we're really choosing in the first place.

How far a given reader gets in this progression depends on how much truth she is prepared to absorb and how many of the poem's details she tries to account for before setting it aside. Hecht doesn't mean to suggest that every successful traversal of the poem must proceed through precisely these phases in precisely this order, and neither do I.

We find a similar bit of blow-softening indirection in an enigmatic little poem brought to my attention by James Longenbach.[18]

Best Things dwell out of Sight
The Pearl - the Just - Our Thought -

Most shun the Public Air
Legitimate, and Rare -

The Capsule of the Wind
The Capsule of the Mind

18. It was a favorite of Harold Bloom's as well, though it left Bloom uncharacteristically speech-less. See Bloom, *The Daemon Knows*, 200–201.

Exhibit here, as doth a Burr -
Germ's Germ be where?

(Fr 1012, J 998; 1865)

This time we have two conspicuously stationed slant rhymes to follow up and think through: "Sight"/"Thought" and "Wind"/"Mind"

Longenbach treats the poem as a tantalizing set of exercises in
imagining things we can't exactly picture—"The Capsule of the
Wind," "Germ's Germ"—rather than as a connected statement. He
concludes by relishing an outrageous pun:

> We are able to conceive of what is hidden in these lines because
> we are able to perceive what is visible. The capsule of the mind
> (the body) is as plainly apprehensible as the burr, and we assume
> the existence of the germ just as we assume the existence of the
> mind. The more exquisite "Germ's Germ" is conceivable because
> we may split the burr to see the germ, and even the daringly
> intangible metaphor of the "Capsule of the Wind" is explicable
> because it is followed by the more readily imagined "Capsule of
> the Mind." Yet the poem is thrilling because the point of these
> metaphors remains partially occluded: the metaphors oscillate
> between allowing us to picture an image (the body) and tempt-
> ing us with the unpicturable (the wind's container) . . .
>
> Concealed in the concluding question . . . is a possibility
> that feels both threatening and enticing: if we could picture the
> "Capsule of the Wind," then the "Germ's Germ ought to beware.[19]

I believe this poem pursues a connected argument about the nature
and career of the things that are by nature best, an argument which
reaches successively more challenging conclusions as it goes, an

19. Longenbach, *The Resistance to Poetry*, 7–8.

argument which divides our assimilation of the poem into successive stages or phases: a Platonic phase, a Homeric phase, and a naturalist phase.

Platonic Phase. The conspicuous inclusion of "thought" and "the Just" in the list of Legitimate and Rare things suggests we should commence our reading in a vaguely Platonic frame of mind. Suppose certain special Legitimate and Rare things are by their nature better than common things and the source or seed or Germ of the more qualified goodness these common things manage to muster. Such special things naturally shun the Public Air, keep to themselves, whether to protect their own purity or out of sheer proud self-sufficiency.

Yet if such things are to exhibit and exercise their excellence, they need space in which to do so and something to breathe while they do so—a Private Air. And this Private Air needs to be cordoned off from the ambient Public Air by an enclosing barrier or Capsule, surrounding and protecting the Rare things as a Burr surrounds and protects a seed or an oyster surrounds and protects a Pearl.

Insofar as we spectators encounter and contemplate and enjoy such things, we are with them even now "here," *inside* the relevant Capsule or Capsules. But where is that, precisely? Where is "here"?

The question becomes even more pressing if one supposes some *single* special thing, a Best of the Best and Rarest of the Rare, a Form of the Good, a Supremely Perfect Being, a Germ's Germ, is the *ultimate* source of whatever more qualified goodness common things manage to muster. Where—within what sort of Capsule—might we encounter a thing like *that?*

In "what is outside heaven," "a place beyond heaven," says Socrates in the *Phaedrus:*

> ... When the souls we call immortals reach the top, they move outward and take their stand on the high ridge of heaven, where

its circular motion carries them around as they stand while they gaze upon what is outside heaven.

The place beyond heaven—none of our earthly poets has ever sung or will ever sing its praises enough! . . . What is in this place is without color and without shape and without solidity, a being that really is what it is, the subject of all true knowledge, visible only to intelligence, the soul's steersman.[20]

This is usually read as a rejection of the "where" question rather than a serious answer to it—a declaration by Plato that the very Best things, the Forms, neither have nor need locations. Be that as it may, *for the poem I am reading now,* everything excellent has a place from which to exhibit and exercise its excellence: the place where it is. So *for this poem,* the question of where we are remains alive and pressing.

Homeric Phase. This question refers us back to the couplet that fascinates Longenbach:

The Capsule of the Wind
The Capsule of the Mind

How are we to take the word "of" in these formulations? Are we to consider the Capsule *that is* the Wind, the Capsule *that is* the Mind? In that case the Wind on the one hand and the Mind on the other are (metaphorical) Capsules serving to (metaphorically) contain Rare things. The *ofs* would be on all fours with the *ofs* in "Now is the winter *of* our discontent / Made glorious summer by this Sun *of* York." It is natural enough and traditional enough to think of the Mind as a container for Thought, and Thought appears on Dickinson's initial list of Rarities. But though Wind can carry or embody things as Legitimate

20. Plato, *Phaedrus,* 247c.

and Rare by Dickinson's own standards as song and speech, it doesn't *contain* them in any obvious sense.

So we are to consider instead the Capsule that *contains* the Wind and the Capsule that *contains* the Mind. Wind and Mind are themselves among the Legitimate and Rare things in need of Capsules. It is natural enough or traditional enough to think of the Body as containing the Mind. But how could anything contain the Wind? Isn't the Wind our paradigm of what *can't* be caught or contained, even if it is harnessed nowadays as a renewable energy source? There's a tradition to the contrary, according to which King Aeolus gave Odysseus a bag containing all the winds, a bag Odysseus' crew heedlessly opened at an inopportune time, to disastrous effect (see *Odyssey* 10). What remains true, even if we take Aeolus' bag seriously, is that Wind can't exhibit and exercise its characteristic excellences while bagged up or otherwise encapsulated. I can't confine Wind and still let Wind be Wind. Putting Wind on our list of Legitimate and Rare things puts pressure on the idea that Capsules afford such things a closed sphere of activity distinct from themselves, a Private Air.

Naturalist Phase. This brings us at last to "Burs"—Burrs—and how it is that they contain and exhibit "Germs." A Burr is a seedcase with prickles, prickles that function defensively (to keep the seed from getting eaten) and offensively (to help it hitch a ride to new surroundings on the fur or clothing of some passing animal or human).

Unless prematurely cut open, a Burr doesn't "exhibit" the seed within until it ceases to protect it, ceases to carry it, ceases to encapsulate it—by exposing it to ordinary Public Air after all. (Think of a germinating Beechnut or Horse Chestnut.) Which is as it should be, since it is in the Public Air, the only Air there really is, that the Germ within finally expresses itself and fulfills itself *as* a Germ, by germinating. The Capsules in which seeds are sheathed, Burrs, protect them from a premature death by consumption and transport them to promising new surroundings by enlisting the help of unwilling and uncomprehending bystanders. They then fall away, so that the seeds within can fulfill themselves as seeds by transforming themselves into growing plants.

If this is how Best things typically work and how they typically make use of Capsules that from time to time protect them and carry them about, so much the worse for their supposed Platonic self-sufficiency. Indeed, so much the worse for *them* (in the long run), since their fulfillment involves their own extinction via eventual exposure to the Public Air. Best things are by their nature such as to express and fulfill their characteristic excellence in a temporally extended process involving their protection (for a while), their dissemination (with the aid of uncomprehending and unwilling intermediaries), and their eventual destruction (via germination, transformation, and death).

If true at all, this conclusion is a *hard* truth—difficult to absorb, difficult to accept, difficult to delight in. Perhaps especially so for Dickinson herself. For Dickinson was the one who renounced and condemned literary investment, literary commerce, "Publication," as "the Auction / Of the Mind of Man" (Fr 788, J 709; 1863). Yet it now appears that Rare Best things *must* attach themselves to uncomprehending strangers if they are to express and fulfill their own excellence. Dickinson was the one who viewed poetry as fulfilling the natural and social phenomena of which it speaks by absorbing them into something better and more self-sufficient. (Vendler calls this her "sacrilegious worship of the Syllable."[21]) As Dickinson put it herself in "The Brain is wider than the Sky - " (Fr 598, J 632; 1863):

> The Brain is just the weight of God -
> For - Heft them - Pound for Pound -
> And they will differ - if they do -
> As Syllable from Sound.

---

21. Vendler, *Dickinson: Selected Poems and Commentaries*, 8.

It turns out that *self-sufficient* excellence and *ultimate* fulfillment are not to be had, in poetry or anywhere else.

So much the worse for the very idea of a Perfect Being, a Form of the Good, a Germ's Germ serving as the enduring and surpassingly excellent source of the more transient and qualified excellence to be found in common things. Germ's Germ, beware!

6.

Dickinson has her own distinctive motives for resorting to figurative language: metaphor, metonymy, personification, and the rest. She uses these figures to hold the world at bay, but she holds the world at bay in order to tell and absorb hard truths about it. Sometimes the truths are subtle and hard to make out; other times they are frightening and hard to confront. On the side of trope, Dickinson attempts to improve our view of important objects by obstructing it. Sometimes this is a matter of enhancing the visibility of subtle features by obscuring more obvious ones. Other times it is a matter of letting less challenging elements of a view prepare us to absorb more challenging ones in the fullness of time, by a kind of blow-cushioning.

On the side of scheme, Dickinson crafts something darting, hesitant, and variably paced from stanzas whose association with the praise of God on the one hand (in hymns) and secular lament on the other (in popular ballads) is so deep and so visceral that individual poems set to work for us as contexts in which to rejoice or contexts in which to grieve, long before we come to terms with the particular truths the poems purport to tell. We know where we are with these forms and their immemorial themes immediately and instinctively. But only up to a point. For Dickinson teaches these forms to dodge and weave, to speed up and slow down, to disturb and destabilize the reassuring first impressions tradition makes them deliver. The slant rhymes, the dashes, the strategically placed short spondaic lines are among the most conspicuous points of disturbance, and accounting for their presence plays an important part in working out what individual poems go on to say. A general terseness speeds up the reading process, so that the poems have time to mean all that they have it in them to mean only after repeated encounters.

Emerson says in "The Poet" that "it is not meters, but a meter-making argument, that makes a poem" (Emerson, 1981, 450). Yet there are things we can come to believe only with the help of poems of an appropriate shape and sound. If there are meter-making arguments, there are also argument-making metrical resources:

> By a departing light
> We see acuter, quite,
> Than by a wick that stays.
> There's something in the flight
> That clarifies the sight
> And decks the rays.
>
> (Fr 1749, J 1714; undated)[22]

REFERENCES

Anderson, Charles R. *Emily Dickinson's Poetry: Stairway of Surprise.* Garden City, NY: Anchor Books, 1966.

Bloom, Harold. *The Daemon Knows: Literary Greatness and the American Sublime.* Oxford: Oxford University Press, 2015.

22. Profound thanks to Oren Izenberg for remarkably detailed, perceptive, and generous comments on an earlier version, and to Paul Woodruff for his suggestion about "serge." Thanks as well to Krista Lawlor, my reader of first and last resort.

Bromwich, David. *Skeptical Music: Essays on Modern Poetry.* Chicago and London: University of Chicago Press, 2001.

Emerson, Ralph Waldo. *Essays and Lectures* New York: Library of America, 1981.

Franklin, R. W., ed. *The Poems of Emily Dickinson.* Reading ed. Cambridge, MA, and London: Belknap Press, Harvard University, 1999.

Hecht, Anthony. "The Riddles of Emily Dickinson" *New England Review* 1, no. 1 (1978): 1–24.

Hollander, John. *Rhyme's Reason: A Guide to English Verse.* New, enlarged ed. New Haven and London: Yale University Press, 1989.

Hollander, John. *Vision and Resonance: Two Senses of Poetic Form.* 2nd ed. New Haven: Yale University Press, 1985.

Howe, Susan. *My Emily Dickinson.* Berkeley: North Atlantic Books, 1985.

Johnson, Thomas H., ed. *The Letters of Emily Dickinson.* Cambridge, MA, and London: Belknap Press, Harvard University, 1955.

Johnson, Thomas H., ed. *The Complete Poems of Emily Dickinson.* Boston: Little, Brown, 1960.

Longenbach, James. *The Resistance to Poetry.* Chicago and London: University of Chicago Press, 2004.

Longenbach, James. *The Virtues of Poetry.* Minneapolis: Graywolf Press, 2013.

Montaigne, Michel de. *The Complete Essays.* Translated by M. A. Screech. London and New York: Penguin Books, 2003.

Plato. *Phaedrus.* Translated by Alexander Nehamas and Paul Woodruff. Indianapolis: Hackett, 1995.

Plato. *Republic.* Translated by C. D. C. Reeve. Indianapolis: Hackett, 2004.

Riskin, Jessica. *The Restless Clock: A History of the Centuries-Long Argument over What Makes Living Things Tick.* Chicago and London: University of Chicago Press, 2016.

Sewall, Richard B. *The Life of Emily Dickinson.* Cambridge, MA: Harvard University Press, 1994.

Vendler, Helen. *Dickinson: Selected Poems and Commentaries.* Cambridge, MA, and London: Harvard University Press, 2010.

Wolff, Cynthia Griffin. *Emily Dickinson.* Reading, MA: Addison-Wesley, 1988.

Chapter 6

Dickinson and Pivoting Thought

EILEEN JOHN

... I remembered that I, myself, in my smaller way, sang off charnel steps. Every day life feels mightier, and what we have the power to be, more stupendous.[1]

Dickinson's poems often present a kind of epistemic predicament: we have limited knowledge but also expansive awareness. Within the scope of our limited experience and understanding there is nonetheless a potentially overwhelming complexity. Dwelling on either aspect—the extent and nature of our ignorance or the prospects for comprehending what we are aware of—has the power to undermine or stymie thought. It is also a problem for action more broadly speaking. If I have an ongoing combination of ignorance and ill-managed content concerning reality, how can I understand my constraints and options, form sensible goals, or act responsibly? Can I know what I am doing? Though it does not seem promising to argue that Dickinson has a single way of responding to this predicament, I want to articulate one kind of response that I find in her work. It is a relatively constructive response, in the sense that it does not doom us to being overwhelmed and stymied. It is also, I hope, interesting in the way that it handles the ignorance and complexity. The images and metaphors that I will highlight are Dickinson's hinges and seams.

1. From Emily Dickinson 1864 letter to Louise and Fanny Norcross (L298).

The Poetry of Emily Dickinson. Elisabeth Camp, Oxford University Press (2021). © Oxford University Press.
DOI: 10.1093/oso/9780190651190.003.0007

When her poems incorporate these mechanisms for linking materials and planes, they suggest a structure for being oriented in multiple
dimensions without full grasp of or immersion in all of them at once.
The transition evoked in the letter quoted earlier the poet singing off
charnel steps, is an example of the kind of multiple orientation that
she explores. The poet can have a foot in song and in the most brute
bodily debris of life. Being positioned in that way does not mean that
there is a seamless mutual intelligibility between the two domains,
but, if the seam or hinge structure works, the domains are linkable in
a way that generates "tension" of some kind. They can be experienced
as "pulling" in importantly different directions, and this is a state that
can encompass multiplicity and failures of knowledge, without suc-
cumbing to paralysis or oblivion.

This line of thought incorporates ideas that are at work in
other philosophically focused accounts of Dickinson. Deppman
notes Dickinson's "wide variety of figures for mental failure,
non-knowledge, and inexplicability," while also referring to her
"knowledgeable flexibility."[2] Tursi links Dickinson to a pragmatist commitment to "retaining systems of metaphysical and social
interconnectivity within epistemological uncertainty."[3] Deppman
and Tursi explore the potential for reading Dickinson in pragmatic
terms, Deppman drawing on Richard Rorty's pragmatic ironism
and Tursi on William James's pragmatism. My line of thought
benefits from their readings while also skirting some of the commitments they entail. Very roughly, I take the hinges and seams
to be more earnest than ironic as achievements, and the pragmatist orientation around human needs and goals does not seem
fully in sync with Dickinson's openness to leveling the human
and non-human perspectives. As will be apparent, however, I am

2. Deppman, *Trying to Think with Emily Dickinson*, 108.
3. Tursi, "Emily Dickinson, Pragmatism, and the Conquests of Mind," 152.

circling around many of the same delicate issues, concerning how Dickinson conceives of human thought and activity developing in a non-arbitrary, meaningful way, without assuming a unifying and confidently ordered structure of knowledge.

CAN WE KNOW WHAT TO THINK?

Here are two poems that highlight a grand failure—of knowledge, thought, or expression—but also show a resistance to being diminished by it.

I found the words to every thought
I ever had - but One -
And that - defies me -
As a Hand did try to chalk the Sun

To Races - nurtured in the Dark -
How would your own - begin?
Can Blaze be shown in Cochineal -
Or Noon - in Mazarin?

(Fr 436, J 581; 1862)

The Missing All - prevented Me
From missing minor Things.
If nothing larger than a World's
Departure from a Hinge -
Or Sun's extinction, be observed -
'Twas not so large that I
Could lift my Forehead from my work
For Curiosity.

(Fr 995, J 985; 1865)

There is something big, comprehensively big, that cannot be expressed or known: the All is missed, the "One" thought cannot be formulated. But words are found for *every other* thought, and "Me" manages not to miss the huge pool of "minor Things" that fall short of the World's Departure or Sun's extinction. These poems both end with images or acknowledgments of absorption in forms of comparatively minor activity. The suddenly specific, exotic words for red and blue—"Cochineal" and "Mazarin" deriving from the names for far-flung insects—evoke vibrant, precise experience and effort at expression.[4] In "The Missing All," the claim of the minor things seems secure, even if there is a failure of explanatory comprehension at the highest level. The poem ends with the image of a person bent over her work, not lifting her "Forehead." Is it curiosity that keeps her at her work, or is curiosity the force that fails to get her to leave it aside to turn to larger things? The latter suggestion, that speculative curiosity is too weak and that something stronger binds her to her work, seems to make most sense of the syntax in those final lines. But it also seems clear that there is curiosity for "All" *somehow* motivating this thinker and worker. She is not uninterested in the big, comprehensive explanation, but the lack of it is not debilitating.

This is one of the poems that has a "Hinge" explicitly present, in "a World's / Departure from a Hinge - " in the middle of the poem. It is an odd, image-built idea. If the world departs on a hinge, then it is not really gone, it has just swung out of view or, less visually, it is

---

4. Addressing "races nurtured in the dark" is likely to strike us as a denigrating reference, but I am not sure what distinction Dickinson aims for (race, religion, geography?) or if she includes herself in the dark. The stanza at least seems to pose a genuine question, not assert superiority. Linda Freedman links these races to Plato's cave-dwellers, who only get "second-hand" experience: "To have a thought is equivalent to knowing the sun; to hear about it is only comparable to seeing a rough and primitive drawing, or a flickering shadow thrown upon the cave's wall" (Freedman, *Emily Dickinson and the Religious Imagination*, 5). I take the fact that the supposed primitive cave-dwellers have wonderful names for the colors of beetles and butterflies to be rather a challenge to Plato's priorities.

at a different angle or orientation from where we started with it. This would still be wildly disturbing, but it would not be an annihilation of the world. Maybe the "Hinge," the mechanism that somehow allows for different angles, would remain accessible. It is that kind of aware- ness that I think Dickinson is interested in, with an insistence on beginning or continuing work while failing to reach the big thought. We might think that the justification of our commitments and grasp of how to go on living needs to rest on, say, comprehension of the Good or God or an all-encompassing ideal, but these poems seem to testify to the viability of ongoing smaller projects. There are other things worth not missing, and we are capable of not missing them, within the absorbing work and varied colors and categories at hand.

Let me briefly note two other readings that highlight similar fea- tures in Dickinson but consider them part of a more overwhelmed, stymied, or passive stance. Anne-Lise François includes Dickinson in a lineage of authors and texts that "locate fulfilment not in narrative fruition but in grace, understood both as a simplicity or slightness of formal means and as a freedom from work."[5] These figures offer an ethos of "minimal contentment" or "minimal realization," coun- tering rationalist and aesthetic ideals with "something more modest, wearier, and less redemptive."[6,7] François's emphasis on Dickinson as failing to depict progressive, educative, redemptive narratives seems on target, but the model of narrative progress and fulfilment does not exhaust the possibilities for identifying immodest, even "mighty" activity (in the vocabulary of the previous letter as embodied or

---

5. François, *Open Secrets*, xvi.

6. François, *Open Secrets*, xix, xix.

7. See readings of specific poems as, e.g., setting "aside illusions about the difference 'complete knowledge' can make," annulling "the possibility of a morally educative *peripeteia*," express- ing "the uninflected passage from possession to destitution or ... from as yet unmet possibil- ity to its simple disappearance," and marking "the growing downward of 'something passiver' out of hope's own passiveness" (François, *Open Secrets*, 173, 177, 179—the last passage quot- ing Dickinson's "A Prison gets to be a friend").

celebrated in the poetry. Especially through consideration of some poems focusing on work, I will suggest that Dickinson is able to find in the routines and competence involved in working life some immodest achievements and forms of knowledge.

Ted Hughes, introducing a selection of Dickinson's poems, also emphasizes the powerful negatives—the stymied, stricken, withdrawn attitudes—that can be found in Dickinson. He takes her to have had a deep and terrible vision that was "like a contradiction to everything that the life in her trusted and loved, it was almost a final revelation of horrible Nothingness."

> Remaining true to this, she could make up her mind about nothing. It stared through her life. It stared out of every smallest thing and gave the world its awesome, pathetic importance. Registering everywhere and in everything the icy chill of its nearness, she did not know what to think. . . . In its light, all other concerns floated free of finality, became merely relative, susceptible to her artistic play.[8]

Here Hughes reads Dickinson almost as an early postmodernist, uncommitted and floating in the face of what he calls her "Holy Trinity": "whatever it was that lay beyond her frightening vision, and the crowded, beloved Creation around her, and Death."[9] Hughes further offers this vivid account of her poetic practice:

> There is the slow, small metre, a device for bringing each syllable into close-up, as under a microscope; there is the deep, steady focus, where all the words lie in precise and yet somehow free relationships, so that the individual syllables are on the point of

---

8. Hughes, "Introduction to *A Choice of Emily Dickinson's Verse*," 358–359.
9. Hughes, "Introduction to *A Choice of Emily Dickinson's Verse*," 359.

slipping into utterly new meanings, all pressing to be uncovered;
there is the mosaic, pictogram concentration of ideas; there is
the tranced suspense and deliberation in her punctuation of
dashes . . . the freakish blood-and-nerve paradoxical vitality of
her latinisms; the musical games—of opposites, parallels, mirrors, chinese puzzles, harmonizing and counterpointing whole
worlds of reference; and everywhere there is the teeming carni-
val of world-life.[10]

I take this account to summon up a different sense of her poetry,
not the mood of an "icy chill" but something intricately absorbing
and lively. Perhaps such poetry, in which "words lie in precise and
yet somehow free relationships," or "whole worlds of reference" are
brought into harmony and counterpoint, could indeed manifest not
knowing what to think, with the forms of mobility signaling an inability to fix on thoughts and on what is worth thinking: complexity and
uncertainty win out. The more positive spin I will put on the poetic
data is not offered in a conclusive spirit—there is too much going on
in this poetry. But I do want to explore a model of thinking that I find
in numerous Dickinson poems, with the guiding ideas that there are
radically different kinds of thought and that a human being can move
between them with some competence. Words themselves, relating
to each other precisely but—somehow—freely, can mark hinging
or pivoting points that characterize this kind of thought. Words can
show where we can pivot between different meaning-bearing dimensions and contexts.[11]

10. Hughes, "Introduction to *A Choice of Emily Dickinson's Verse*," 359.
11. Morag Harris explores the idea that individual words in Dickinson are vehicles of
    thought: "Both Coleridge and Dickinson discuss the issue of one "word" or sign symboliz-
    ing/evoking multiple things and all their relationships" (Harris, *Linguistic Transformations*,
    22). Harris is also very interesting on "hinge" relations in Dickinson, "mapping the meeting-
    and-parting points of component elements," as "'feasible distinctions,' not 'hardened
    dichotomies'" (75). J. H. Prynne says thought, in Dickinson, "may be present by means of

DEATH AND HOUSEWORK

One shift of context that Dickinson returns to many times is the shift between life and death. Her poems try out numerous perspectives on that transition and the resulting divide between the living and the dead.[12] What being dead is, and what it is like, if anything, to be dead, is one of the central limitations of our knowledge. We know that we die, but being dead seems to be a state we have no informative access to. Death, then, seems like a blank wall that we run into; there is not a way to "pivot" in thought so as to be knowledgeably or competently oriented toward it. I want to consider one of Dickinson's poems that deals with the dead-living divide and that might seem to occupy or accept this stymied position. "How many times these low feet staggered" addresses the occasion of a housewife's death. The woman's life is evoked through reference to her housework and the unacknowledged effort she gave to it.

How many times these low feet staggered
Only the soldered mouth can tell -
Try - can you stir the awful rivet -
Try - can you lift the hasps of steel!

Stroke the cool forehead - hot so often
Lift - if you care - the listless hair -
Handle the adamantine fingers
Never a thimble - more - shall wear -

little or no argument... with origins implicit in gaps and silences between often apparently simple words.... the expression of enlarged reaction in the reader (even, a kind of sublimity) is provoked initially by sudden localised shifts of reference within the poem's structure, by heroic and sometimes giddy extension of perspective" (Prynne, "Poetic Thought," 606).

12. E.g., "I heard a Fly buzz - when I died," "Because I could not stop for Death," "I never hear that one is dead," "I've seen a Dying Eye," "If anybody's friend be dead."

Buzz the dull flies - on the chamber window -
Brave - shines the sun through the freckled pane -
Fearless - the cobweb swings from the ceiling -
Indolent Housewife - in Daisies - lain!

(Fr 238, J 187; 1861)

In line with François's approach to Dickinson, this is not a poem that offers or hints at a life story of redemption or progress. To the extent that her life is portrayed, we learn that she exhausted herself keeping flies and dust at bay, and that her efforts are quickly, effortlessly undone after her death. The first stanza gives a disturbing image of death soldering her mouth shut and imprisoning her, as if within a suit of armor. It is true that the poem ends with a surprisingly cheerful image of her lying in daisies, but that image is part of the strange rupture of her death—her body buried, destined to merge with the soil and plant life—rather than an intelligible outcome of her own life's activity. The question of whether her labor was worthwhile, whether she had good reason to spend her life mending, washing, and the rest, seems not to be posed, perhaps set aside as not likely to get an encouraging answer.

Granted that the poem records the dissolution of a wearying life, is the force of the poem itself resigned, weary, modest? Let me make two claims, one broad and one slightly fussy, about what Dickinson does in this poem. The three stanzas are each quite different in mood and focus: the first is dramatic and dreadful in its imagery of the staggering feet and the now sealed-off life; the second will not leave the body alone and dwells intrusively on the lost feel of skin, hair, and hands; and the third breezily notes the encroachment of oblivious flies, sunshine, daisies, and non-living (but swinging!) cobwebs. The sum of these parts is not knowledge of "what it is like to be dead," answering our fearful questions, but it is an unflinching survey of aspects of death that we do know about. The poem shifts through different "worlds of reference" relevant to acknowledging death, from the finally inaccessible and perhaps never expressed experience of the dead person, to the loss of intimacy and interaction for "you" still living, to the many beings and processes for which the death is not a loss and makes no mark as an event. The impact of the life is not grasped or weighed in the same way, or in a steadily evolving way, across the stanzas. That could signal the onset of chaos, but I think it is the ambition of the poem that we hold these aspects of death side by side and find that we have "hinges" that let us swing, grudgingly, between these aspects. The reason the final stanza is powerful is that it stretches the putative life story as far as possible away from the labor and suffering of a person, but the path taken by the body indeed stretches between those poles. The drama, gruesomeness, and insouciance appropriate to the various aspects have those qualities because of the others—the gruesome sensation of a living body become mere thing and the oblivious insouciance of the daisies have those meanings only as counterweights to.the passionate experience of the life. That's the broad point: adequacy to death involves different vanishing points, as it were, that do not follow out the meaning of death in shared terms, but in acknowledging one we do not lose all contact with the others.

To illustrate the detailed workings of the poem, and the hinge-like or pivoting functions of specific words, consider these lines in the second stanza: "Lift - if you care - the listless hair - / Handle the adamantine fingers." The phrase "if you care" is able to summon up two other phrases via "care": "if you can" and "if you dare."[13] It is an accident of English that it can do that, but such accidents are poetic resources. "Care" itself suggests both what one wishes to do and the concern felt for another, and there is a hint of reproach here—perhaps you already do not wish to touch this hair, and perhaps your

13. Vendler, *Dickinson: Selected Poems and Commentaries*, 77.

concern has already evaporated. But the specific caring for the living person that gripped "you" has to dissipate. In letting what one can and dares to do also be heard as alternatives, "care" efficiently evokes the radical transition the witness has to undergo. Of course it remains physically possible to lift hair, but it cannot be a comforting gesture. Touching the dead body begins to become a taboo intimacy, and it may take boldness simply to attend to the reality of the body. In the care-can-dare pivot the changes in what can be done and cared about, what needs to fall away, what can be experienced and known—are identified at once. I think that "Handle" in the next line has a similar effect, in the way it evokes both holding a hand and dealing with a handle, an object unable to return one's grasp. The mourner loses the malleable warmth and responsiveness of the woman's hand, and the interactive pressure of her ordinary presence.

A question that lingers concerns the work involved in this house-wifely life. As suggested above, the poem does not seem to celebrate the inherent value of the work that gave the life, for purposes of the poem, its identity. The poem opens up vantage-points—of eternity, of the steady advances of dust and decomposition—from which the unstinting labor of keeping a household clean and orderly seems to lose point. If the staggering "low feet" refer to the poet's feet as well, there is a parallel question for steady poetic output, which, like fend-ing off household neglect, is not demanded by any cosmic impera-tive.[14] This is a juncture at which the larger failures of knowledge—is it really over when I die? does what I do fit into a grand design? is

14. See Miller, "How 'Low Feet' Stagger": "The staggering 'low feet' of weakness, read differ-ently, become the staggering 'low feet' of poetic power" (135). More broadly, Miller argues that "Dickinson attempts to build up the possibilities of personal choice and control in her poems [. . .]. The poet attempts formally to create that fragile equilibrium in which two forces—a man and a woman, a personal weakness and a strength, the norm and the singu-lar, or a word's grammatical, lexical rules and its metaphorical meanings—attain a tempo-rary reciprocity" (134).

there a God or Good that gives point to all of this?—can cast a pall over the miscellany of choices and activities that fill up a life. One way to adapt to this is to let the human terms—what we need, find satisfying, can conceive of—be the terms that matter. Tursi, in developing a pragmatist approach to Dickinson, gives a nicely balanced sense of what this comes to as a solution or adaptation to our uncertainty. On the one hand, in various poems (as here Tursi comments on "How many schemes may die"), Dickinson gives "the underbelly of pragmatic contingency . . . an unflinching look:"

> Nothing here could be predicted. But it is human attention to this or that detail and the resulting decision that shapes all. This human power carries no triumph or joy or quiet satisfaction, not even when it saves a life. Also absent is the optimism that could accompany the sense that anything is possible. Rather, while it is difficult to say whether the speaker views this universe as indifferent, the schemes themselves have a leveled equality. . . . The moral quality here is up to us. If there is free will, then we are responsible; however blindly, we must proceed.[15]

On the other hand, if blindly and without triumph, the work of human attention and decision is central to reality: "we come to know or understand what we know through a series of choices about this moment or that one. There is a chance that a transcendental whole does indeed exist, but if so, it will do so only because we experience it as a result of a need for it."[16]We can "delimit the chaos into some

15. Tursi, "Emily Dickinson, Pragmatism, and the Conquests of Mind," 156–157.

16. Tursi, "Emily Dickinson, Pragmatism, and the Conquests of Mind," 164. See Tursi on "The Outer - from the Inner": "for her, the 'Inner' is the true origin of all that transpires. It acts upon the outer, not the other way around. But not as a changer; the inner pragmatically creates the outer. The outer forces . . . provide the raw sensory materials, but we compose the picture. The result is 'precise' for being the real thing of the seer—'the inner Brand'" (Tursi, "Emily Dickinson, Pragmatism, and the Conquests of Mind," 163).

kind of personally or socially agreed upon line in the sand as a first stop to a program of action—a conquest by way of the mind's own authority."[17] The mood may not be that of conquest, but the framework implicitly affirmed puts human interests and actions, and the mind's work on their behalf, at the center.

When focusing on the work of a poet, there is no way to avoid the prioritization of human delimiting, composing, and choosing activity. A poem cannot help but embody and affirm the reality of such activity. In my claim about Dickinson's pivoting moves, I too am highlighting the ambitious conceptualizing and epistemic structures that the poems offer. But I resist putting Dickinson in a fully pragmatic frame because her poems, even if they cannot avoid the "brand" of their human hand, do so much to situate human concerns in a larger world found or presumed to run on other diverse principles.[18] The flies and cobwebs are given prominent places because they "do their own thing" or, in the case of cobwebs, are their own thing despite not being agents at all. The housewife and the poet, and the more abstract person bent over her work in "The Missing All," are absorbed in their activities without being able to center them or single them out as *the* determiners of meaning and value. Here we can see the appeal of a Rortyan pragmatic ironism, in which one abstains from centering, or from being non-ironically committed to, the conceptual, evaluative terms one happens to use.[19] Though Deppman does not simply align Dickinson with this type of pragmatism, and in his title notion, *Trying to Think with Emily Dickinson*, foregrounds the

---

17. Tursi, "Emily Dickinson, Pragmatism, and the Conquests of Mind," 162.
18. See Tursi on "Four Trees - upon a solitary Acre," for the "pragmatic speaker's" role in unifying the scene (Tursi, "Emily Dickinson, Pragmatism, and the Conquests of Mind," 172). I take the poem to be doing its best to mark the intersection of the squirrel, boy, wind, sun, God, and poet around the trees, without prioritizing the poet's composing work.
19. See Rorty's conception of the "liberal ironist" (Rorty, *Contingency, Irony, and Solidarity*, especially Ch. 4).

ongoing positive drive to think in her poetry, he also emphasizes a negative achievement of abstention or hesitation:

> Her "hesitation" does not derive from any arbitrary preference for indeterminacy or obstinate refusal to answer questions; it is a way for her to avoid making the ontological mistakes of strong metaphysics, for example, looking for accurate descriptions and "presence" in a structure of being that denies them.[20]

These pragmatist alternatives help to isolate the difficulty of making room for my claims about Dickinson. I want to say that at least some of her poems find a way to maneuver between human-interests-centered commitment and ironist non-commitment, within the acknowledgment of larger ignorance and uncertainty. My way of locating this room to maneuver is by saying Dickinson affirms some important knowledge of relationships, in which different planes or frameworks "meet" and have some mutual relevance, although we cannot assimilate one to another, unify them, or fully grasp why it is possible for them to meet. In my concluding section, I will discuss two further poems that explore some of these "hinges" or "seams," aiming to show that Dickinson does not use them to embrace either swinging, de-stabilizing movement or the governing power of human connections.

PLAYING, SEWING, AND KNOWING WHAT YOU ARE DOING

Some of the things we can fail to know concern ourselves. What are the roots and consequences of my actions? Do I know what is worth

---

20. Deppman, *Trying to Think with Emily Dickinson*, 203.

doing? To what extent is my activity *mine*, in the sense of being under my control and responsive to my discernment of value? As we have seen within the scope of the staggering "low feet" poem, Dickinson can set such questions aside, perhaps suggesting that they can be hidden (and not well-answered) within the suffering, exhaustion, and social constraints of a working life. In philosophical discourse, these questions take center stage in arguments about agency, free will and determinism, and the epistemology of value. The two poems I will discuss in this section are interesting, in part, because they engage with these questions, but not by considering, for instance, a person questioning how to live or facing a specific morally meaningful choice. Dickinson explores conceptions, and the practical undergoing, of important divides and transitions, such as the movement from not having evaluative discernment to having it. In pivoting between different conceptions that matter to those transitions, we do not end up with full comprehension—e.g., knowing the full nature and value of an action—but we can grasp how different contexts, processes, and kinds of meaning intersect in an action. In one poem the context is quite abstract and metaphorical, and in the other extremely concrete but also metaphorical; the poems come at these questions oddly, from a philosopher's perspective. Nonetheless, I think they get some traction on the issues. Let me grant that it is very difficult to say how a short metaphorical poem gets traction on a philosophical problem; I hope some of the examples from Dickinson are suggestive. My somewhat simple thought is that, to the extent that readers pivot imaginatively, conceptually, and inferentially in response to the poems' language and structure, they get an experience of some complex philosophical relationships. That kind of experience does not settle the adequacy and justificatory questions that philosophers pose, but the experientially traced relations are not irrelevant to adequacy and justification either. Part of the appropriate testing of a philosophical view is whether it has some perspicuous bearing on what we do and do not understand, and Dickinson's poems strike me as often providing images and ideas that illuminate what we need to be perspicuous about.

In "We play at Paste," learning to discern value, which is also a process of transforming oneself, is the central topic. Like "I found the words to every thought," it is a brief, two-stanza poem in which the second stanza seems to talk back to or re-direct the confidence of the first.

> We play at Paste -
> Till qualified, for Pearl -
> Then, drop the Paste -
> And deem ourself a fool -
>
> The Shapes - though - were similar -
> And our new Hands
> Learned *Gem*-Tactics -
> Practicing *Sands* -
>
> (Fr 282, J 320; 1862)

The first stanza sketches a confident evaluative hierarchy: paste jewels, and our initial pleasure in these imitations, are ultimately to be disdained in relation to pearls and less foolish selves. Playing is lesser than being qualified. The second stanza seems to re-cast the naïve play by linking it to the transformational process of forming a pearl—the learning hands and practicing sands are aligned. The hands learned, wonderfully, "*Gem*-Tactics." Consider that as a pivoting word. The mind and tongue are likely to trip over it, perhaps groping toward 'gymnastics,' 'fantastic,' or 'syntactic' as possibly informative cousins. But it is not obvious what to do with it. Taking the pearl to be an exemplar, it seems gems would be the result of slow, non-tactical activity, initiated unwittingly. Play, if not quite so un-thinking, is also not supposed to be tactical or instrumental. Aren't these precisely contexts without tactics? And of course, this is not a word in the first place! Maybe "*Gem*-Tactics" is not a functioning hinge word at all, but a pleasurably colliding-rebounding impact site. Does the second stanza offer anything that really works to transform the confident dismissal of the first?

The sense and importance of "*Gem*-Tactics" arise in part from the word being a new and willful construction. It registers as at least poetically tactical, something the poem asks us to learn to say before we could know how to think and use it. We will presumably try to join the things that collide in it: the gem as an emblem of perfection and value—think of the Biblical "pearl of great worth" (Matthew 13: 45–46)—tied to a word that speaks of human planning and choice of means to reach ends. The sound of "Tactics" can also summon up what hands are good at, tactility or touch. The first stanza puts the question of our value into the picture; we ourselves are some of the gems in formation, learning to "deem" ourselves properly. A pivoting move that I think "Gem-Tactics" enables is between two states or processes we know are linked: long stretches of unwitting experience, on the one hand, and being "qualified," having taste or competence in judgment of value, on the other. Does the poem offer an explanation of the transition from experience to judgment and taste?[21] It at least offers a complex set of directions for thinking about it, some images and contexts relevant to an explanation, though the pearl-formation metaphor resists construal of this as a process we can take charge of and fully understand. If "Practicing Sands" is the model, that steers us to a cumulative, grinding, polishing process, with a long timeframe in which things go through very gradual mutual adjustments. While that sounds like sheer cause-and-effect, with no role for tactical

---

21. Hume, in "Of the Standard of Taste," affirms the role of practice and comparison in forming the true judge, but he asserts more than explains the route from practice to evaluative discernment.

action, the notions of practice and play, and use of hands, bring in more than unwitting causal impact. There is pleasure-seeking in play, which can initiate preferences, and practicing involves awareness of repetition and change and an emerging ability to control change. Hands again are interesting in this poem, as they are excellent causal impression-takers, but also our most adept manipulators and makers of shapes. With these assorted resources, the second stanza, though less punchy and less resolved, pushes back against the first stanza's clear, even abrupt abandonment of play. It seems that play, whether imitative, foolish, or idly arranging, lets a slow transformation occur, a kind of learning that is not knowledge- or qualification-led, and that we cannot properly notice as it happens. What is in fact a tremendous transition, from impacts with shapes (such as word-shaped things), to discerning, responsive shaping and appreciation, is made with many small, often not acknowledgeable interactions.[22] The "Gem-Tactics" pivot does not mark a successful explanation, or intelligible smoothing out, of the transition, but it makes clearer what we link in making such transitions, offering some constructive terms and models for thinking about the relevant states and processes.

My last poem takes on the voice of a seamstress, someone who presents herself as a competent, discerning agent. The seam rather than the hinge is a structuring image, which, though similarly an image of flexible joining of independent things, has some different associations as well. The detailed stitching that makes a seam is a paradigm of "close work," with thread rather than metal as the joining medium, and it is associated with (if not in reality restricted to) women's labor. What counts as a good seam is also distinctive. The seam faces two ways, and the outer face of it should ideally be

---

22. Miller, "How 'Low Feet' Stagger": "we see that creation is repetitive, ongoing, and that a symmetry evolves in the relation between the poet's new form and her environment or what she is disrupting" (145).

hard to see, while the hidden inner face shows the seam clearly. Another quality of seams that I think is interesting with respect to the notion of pivoting thought is that, in the workings of thread and fabric, the stitches need to have the right tension. The elements of the seam have to pull on each other properly (not too much, not too little, not unevenly) for the seam to be strong and enduring. "Seam" itself is a great pivoting word, with its philosophically provocative homophone "seem." The relation between real and seeming experience is broached at the end of the poem, as the speaker seems to be both dreaming and observing (and critiquing) her merely dreaming sewing. Perhaps the final stanza refuses to let the dream/reality alternatives be a crushing skeptical problem, since the dream scenario seems to be subordinated to the demands of sewing, whether dreaming or awake.[23] I will in any case focus on "so," the poem's other great pivoting word.

> Don't put up my Thread and Needle -
> I'll begin to Sew
> When the Birds begin to whistle -
> Better Stitches - so -
>
> These were bent - my sight got crooked -
> When my mind - is plain
> I'll do seams - a Queen's endeavor
> Would not blush to own -
>
> Hems - too fine for Lady's tracing
> To the sightless Knot -

23. Deppman's readings of numerous poems are relevant and challenging here. He emphasizes Dickinson on the "contact or crisis point between paradigmatic discourses fitfully trying to cohere." Of "I felt a Cleaving in my Mind," he says, there are "two halves of a brain, or two thoughts, next to each other and needing to be sewn together" (Deppman, *Trying to Think with Emily Dickinson*, 97, 99).

Tucks - of dainty interspersion -
Like a dotted Dot -

Leave my Needle in the furrow -
Where I put it down -
I can make the zigzag stitches
Straight - when I am strong -

Till then - dreaming I am sewing
Fetch the seam I missed -
Closer - so I - at my sleeping -
Still surmise I stitch -

(Fr 681, J 617; 1863)

The speaker is at the end of a long day, assuring either a silent critic or herself that her stitching will be better in the morning. From this weary, self-critical position, the speaker veers into speculative and exuberant claims, as she predicts or imagines her finest sewing achievements.[24]

The two uses of "so" are visually like stitches: " - so - " in the first stanza and " - so I - " in the last. They also perfectly echo the verb *to sew*, providing an easy, sound-borne relation as well as the unexpected visual relation, linking "so" to what the speaker is doing or imagining herself doing. But what is connected by linking "so" and "sew"? As I will briefly illustrate, I take the poem to use sewing as a vehicle for examining different kinds of status we have in our own

---

24. See Bennett, "Emily Dickinson and Her American Women Poet Peers," for a strong critique of Dickinson's sewing poems, contrasting them with socially engaged sewing poetry by her 19th-century female peers. Dickinson wanted "to have her cake (use her poems to maintain her connections in the social world) and eat it (write transcendentally; achieve sublimity and immortality) too" (232). However, "this double-sided poetics left traditional gender roles intact and Dickinson batting irresolutely between them" (218). Though without contesting Bennett's specific argument, I am trying to put a more positive spin on some of the "batting between" that the poems offer.

activities—forms of knowledge, control, and appreciation that bind us more or less intelligibly to what we do. "So" turns out to be helpfully flexible in meaning and function for this purpose.

In the first stanza's "Better Stitches - so - " the use of "so" is colloquial and extremely economical. It means, to unpack it slightly, "just so" or "this is how you do it." We might wonder why "so" is able to mean that, but at any rate it is a usage that claims local competence with something shown, some know-how that is perhaps difficult to articulate or not worth articulating. But even this small claim to competence marks some ambitious connections: one has some control over given materials, and the "- so -" conveys confident evaluation of one's own effectiveness. The material input is successfully linked to one's purposive action. The modest effectiveness claimed here is not the same as producing something elegant, beautiful, or dizzyingly fine, as envisioned in the next two stanzas, but I think the relations between these types of achievement, and between the judgments of value they involve, is also one of the pivoting moves the poem makes. The stage of "just so" competence is one of the bases of those aesthetically evaluable achievements. You need to do the basically effective work to get powerful aesthetic effects. As with "We play at Paste," there is a known relation between two kinds of activity, a person's ordinary, practical competence and an artist's pleasurably absorbing, even exhilarating work.[25] They are recognizably distinct achievements, and call for different kinds of satisfaction, but they meet around some shared activity—say, stitching or word use, and the contrasting qualities of either one help illuminate what is distinctive about the other.

25. I find the "sightless Knot" and "Tucks - of dainty interspersion - / Like a dotted Dot -" somehow exhilarating. They present the fineness of the sewn features as outstripping our perceptual abilities. The hems and tucks are humanly sewn, but the patterns and structures emerge from and disappear into features we cannot perceive.

When we reach the final "- so I -," there is an "I" in the stitch. We already have the "just so" reading of "so" and might then read this "so I" in those terms, as a sort of claim to local self-competence: "this is how I am me" or "this is how I do it," namely, whatever I do in being myself. But "so I" also sounds like we are in the middle of an explanation or justification. "So" as a connective can convey something like "I am pausing to note that I am about to go on in a certain way, and to suggest that this can be explained and possibly justified." It is a casual alternative to "therefore" or "thus," and it claims at least minimal orientation—I know in some sense where I have been and where I am going—but it can also gloss over uncertainty as to the kind of intelligibility my continued activity has. It might seem that we would know very well what we are doing when sewing (or otherwise acting) and why, but the poem does not give the "I" that kind of clear, independent confidence. There is unintended "zigzagging," her sight is crooked, and her mind is not plain. In construing this "- so I -" as a pivot word or phrase, I take it to signal, laconically, the very mixed status of a self in the midst of its activities. "I" have some know-how or competence in being me, but I also figure in intersecting processes and contexts that stretch beyond my competence.

This poem and the others discussed offer numerous examples of the kinds of process and context, and differing forms of intelligibility or meaning, that can intersect in a given self. "I" may be "stitched" into the tendencies of unthinkably many things: tiny causal impacts, God's plans, the growth, responsive instincts, and the death of living things, the movements of the earth and sun, the structure of time from individual moments to eternity, and the variously controlled and comprehended activities we ascribe to ourselves (such as perceiving, naming, dreaming, playing, practicing, working, knowing, neglecting, tiring, fulfilling a prescribed social role, experiencing beauty, making a mistake, assessing loss and value, and wondering what to think). It would be reassuring to know how to prioritize these things, and to know what structure of knowledge and hierarchy of goals was demanded or most adequate to this complexity. Dickinson does not offer that kind of reassurance. She is rather fascinated with the multiplicity and with what it is like to be implicated in it. My claim, glancingly supported here, is that Dickinson's poems nonetheless seek and offer structure that is appropriate to the kind of being we have. We can only partially grasp much of what influences us or is at work in us, even in our own capacities for learning and growth. But we can be aware of important joining points, the hinges and seams, e.g., where unwitting and skillful activity converge, or physical patterns support aesthetic delight, or bodies turn into things, or words get attached to colors. Her pivoting words are one way in which this kind of structure can show up in a poem. They mark points at which we can swing to or feel the pull of another relevant context or process. On this model, there will often not be a straightforward account of "what I am doing and why," for example, and that can sound like an admission of philosophical defeat and confusion. However, my further sense of Dickinson's achievement is that, in highlighting the pivoting moves, she affirms our complex possibility space and encourages her readers to acknowledge the relationships and constructive tension between different contexts and bearers of meaning.[26]

REFERENCES

Bennett, Paula Bernat. 2002. "Emily Dickinson and Her American Women Poet Peers." In *The Cambridge Companion to Emily Dickinson*, ed. Wendy Martin, 215–235. Cambridge: Cambridge University Press.

Deppman, Jed. 2008. *Trying to Think with Emily Dickinson*. Amherst: University of Massachusetts Press.

26. Great thanks to Elisabeth Camp and to Antony Aumann, Christina Britzolakis, Richard Eldridge, Rick Antony Furtak, David Hills, Oren Izenberg, Tina Lupton, Emma Mason, Magdalena Ostas, Karen Simecek, and Susan Whitlock.

Dickinson, Emily. 1864. Letter to Louise and Fanny Norcross (L298). Last updated December 16, 1998. http://archive.emilydickinson.org/correspondence/norcross/l298.html

François, Anne-Lise. 2008. *Open Secrets: The Literature of Uncounted Experience.* Stanford: Stanford University Press.

Freedman, Linda. 2011. *Emily Dickinson and the Religious Imagination.* Cambridge: Cambridge University Press.

Hughes, Ted. 2002. "Introduction to *A Choice of Emily Dickinson's Verse*." In *Emily Dickinson: Critical Assessments*, vol. 2, edited by Graham Clarke, 355–359. Mountfield, East Sussex: Helm Information.

Harris, Morag. 2002. *Linguistic Transformations in Romantic Aesthetics from Coleridge to Emily Dickinson.* Lewiston, NY: Edwin Mellen.

Hume, David. 1965. "Of the Standard of Taste." In *Of the Standard of Taste and Other Essays*, edited by John Lenz, 3–24. Upper Saddle River, NJ: Prentice Hall.

Miller, Christanne. 1983. "How 'Low Feet' Stagger: Disruptions of Language in Dickinson's Poetry." In *Feminist Critics Read Emily Dickinson*, edited by Suzanne Juhasz, 134–155. Bloomington: Indiana University Press.

Prynne, J. H. 2010. "Poetic Thought." *Textual Practice* 24(4): 595–606.

Rorty, Richard. 1989. *Contingency, Irony, and Solidarity.* Cambridge: Cambridge University Press.

Tursi, Renée. 2013. "Emily Dickinson, Pragmatism, and the Conquests of Mind." In *Emily Dickinson and Philosophy*, edited by Jed Deppman, Marianne Noble, and Gary Lee Stonum, 151–174. Cambridge: Cambridge University Press.

Vendler, Helen. 2010. *Dickinson: Selected Poems and Commentaries.* Cambridge, MA: Harvard University Press.

INDEX

For the benefit of digital users, indexed terms that span two pages (e.g., 52–53) may, on occasion, appear on only one of those pages.